ENTRY-LEVEL
LIFE

ENTRY-LEVEL
LIFE

A COMPLETE GUIDE TO MASQUERADING AS A MEMBER OF THE REAL WORLD

DAN ZEVIN

BANTAM BOOKS

NEW YORK · TORONTO · LONDON · SYDNEY · AUCKLAND

ENTRY-LEVEL LIFE

A Bantam Book / May 1994

BOOK DESIGN BY ALEXANDER KNOWLTON.

Illustrations on section openings, in Contents, and on page 17 by Elwood H. Smith. Illustrations on pages 10–11, 32, 69, 75, 79 by Natasha Lessnik. Illustrations on pages 18, 33, 58–59, 77 by Michael Sloan. All photographs courtesy H. Armstrong Roberts except: page 31 by Edward Santalone; page 9 photo of Ross Perot © Mark Reinstein 1992/FPG International; page 9 photo of San Francisco © 1989 Gerald L. French/FPG International; photos on pages 35 and 56 by Alexander Knowlton.

Library of Congress Cataloging-in-Publication Data

Zevin, Dan.

Entry-level life : a complete guide to masquerading as a member of

the real world / Dan Zevin.

p.   cm.

ISBN 0-553-37348-X

I. Title.

PN6162.Z48   1994

646.7'00207—dc20   93-39517

CIP

Published simultaneously in the United States and Canada

Bantam Books are published by Bantam Books, a division of Bantam Doubleday Dell Publishing Group, Inc. Its trademark, consisting of the words "Bantam Books" and the portrayal of a rooster, is Registered in U.S. Patent and Trademark Office and in other countries. Marca Registrada. Bantam Books, 1540 Broadway, New York, New York 10036.

PRINTED IN THE UNITED STATES OF AMERICA

RRH   0 9 8 7 6 5 4 3 2 1

DEDICATION

To the ever
Real-Worldly
MEGAN TINGLEY,
who never once
during the
course of this
project said,
"Can I have
that ten bucks
you owe me?"

ACKNOWLEDGMENTS

Many thanks to all the Entry-Level Lifers who contributed, knowingly and unknowingly, to the contents of this book. Special thanks to the members (past, present, and honorary) of the highly prestigious Somerville Writers' Colony: Stephanie Booth, Sari Boren, Brian Burgoon, Esther Craine, Stephanie Gruner, Miriam Levinson, Adam Lichtenstein, Erica Lombard, Dan Ochnsner, Jay Salpecker, Ethan Seidman, John Simons, Joe Strouse, Keith Summa, Megan Tingley, Ian Woodbury, and Allyson Zevin.

I'm also grateful to Superagent Jennifer Rudolph Walsh at the Virginia Barber Literary Agency and Supereditor Jennifer Hershey at Bantam.

Finally, thanks to my parents, Ron Zevin and Linda Zevin, for their encouragement and understanding, particularly their understanding of the following statement: *All of the characters portrayed in this book are ficticious. Any similarity to real persons, living or dead, is coincidental and not intended by the author.*

III. ENTRY-LEVEL OFFICE LIFE 65

CONTENTS

INTRODUCTION

Entry-Level Orientation

YOUR POST COLLEGIATE ROLE:
INSTA-GROWNUP

So, you're out of college! Who knows? Maybe you've even graduated. With your illustrious academic life behind you, it's time to embrace the destiny that lies ahead. A life in which you no longer cram six months of work into one night, fueled by No Doz, Jolt!, and that highly energizing fear of a negative GPA. A life in which you wake up each day *before* the sun sets (and in an identifiable location). A life in which job attendance is mandatory, and the calendar does not revolve in cycles beginning in September and ending in May. *Welcome* to Entry-Level Life.

Do not be alarmed. If you are like most Entry-Level Lifers, you're probably feeling like a fraud in your new role as Insta-Grownup. Neo-Adolescent may be more your frame of mind, especially after being forced to appear in public dressed in that ill-fitting cap and gown. You've now entered the adolescence of adulthood, however—those awkward postcollege years which find you caught somewhere between carefree, Hacky-Sacking youth and responsible, sensible-shoes-wearing adult. Equipped only with your knowledge of pygmy tribal rituals, iambic pentameter, and the other highly practical information you would have acquired in college had you ever attended class, you've suddenly "commenced" into a strange and foreign land known as the Real World.

Relax! All you have to do now is decide what to do with the rest of your life, move to an unfamiliar city, find an apartment, search for roommates, throw them out when you realize they are psychotic, get a job, pay your bills, make new friends, and meet that special Entry-Level someone with whom you'll settle down for the rest of your life. To prevent a premature nervous breakdown, take care of small matters before you proceed:

THINGS TO DO BEFORE READING THIS BOOK

1. Drive cross-country
2. Backpack through Europe
3. Sow your wild oats
4. Find yourself[1]

Once you've completed this prerequisite coursework, you'll be ready to conquer the more complex challenges of your Entry-Level Life: faking a résumé; getting a Xerox machine to sort, stack, *and* staple 3,000 copies for your violently insane boss; surviving that traumatic transition from dorm to dump, and from keg party to cocktail party.

By following the advice dispensed in these pages, you are going to become a productive, respectable citizen of the Real World.[2] The key (as the highly paid blowhard who gave your college commencement speech neglected to mention) is simply to pretend you know what you're doing.

[1] *Hint: You are somewhere in the proximity of this book.*
[2] *You may also end up behind bars.*

SECTION

I

Entry-Level Housing

YOUR NEW LEARNING ENVIRONMENT

Where to live after graduation is a decision the Entry-Level Lifer should not take lightly or without several Long Island iced teas. Of course, you could opt exclusively for the iced teas. In this case, you will probably decide to stay in your comfortable college town, where you've already got plenty of pals and an exciting faxing job lined up in the graduate department of actuarial studies. The risk is waking up one day to find you are a thirty-two-year-old embarrassment who still attends Stigma Stigma Stigma parties in a stained college sweatshirt you've long since outgrown.

Another option is to move to wherever your boyfriend or girlfriend will be living.[1] This is not a bad idea, as it effectively reduces the high phone-sex bills incurred in long-distance relationships. Finally, you may end up relocating for the one job you were offered, in which case it doesn't matter where you live since you'll only see it on your lunch break.

Clearly, the best idea is to choose a thriving metropolis with plenty of jobs in your chosen field, affordable housing, and stimulating nightlife. Due to the fact that this place exists only in the demented minds of college career counselors, base your decision on more specific criteria: How often do you have to move your car? What time is last call? How long is the wait in the unemployment line?

ACCEPTABLE REAL-WORLD CITIES

What qualifies as a Real-World city? Let us first consider what a Real-World city is not. A Real-World city is not a place where you move strictly to pursue one of the following activities: skiing, surfing, substance abusing. These options should, however, be reasonably accessible.

[1] *until you get there*

CITIES OF THE

Real-World city:
NEW YORK

TYPICAL RESIDENT: pale, chain-smoking commercial artist; escaped convict

MAJOR ATTRACTION: twenty-four-hour Korean delis

MAJOR DETRACTION: murderous bike messengers

POSTCOLLEGIATE PASTIME: working weekends

OFFICIAL CITY MOTTO: "Get outta my fuckin' way."

WHERE YOU'LL LIVE AFTER ONE MONTH'S RENT RENDERS YOU HOMELESS: Bed-Stuy

Real-World city:
SEATTLE

TYPICAL RESIDENT: secretly neurotic wearer of politically correct sports sandals

MAJOR ATTRACTION: intravenous caffeine clinics

MAJOR DETRACTION: freshly detoxed L.A. expatriates

POSTCOLLEGIATE PASTIME: canvassing for Greenpeace

OFFICIAL CITY MOTTO: "Not just another Nirvana."

WHERE YOU'LL LIVE AFTER ONE MONTH'S RENT RENDERS YOU HOMELESS: Kent

Real-World city:
CHICAGO

TYPICAL RESIDENT: lost convention-goer wearing "Hello My Name Is…" sticker

MAJOR ATTRACTION: blues bars

MAJOR DETRACTION: rednecks

POSTCOLLEGIATE PASTIME: stalking professional athletes

OFFICIAL CITY MOTTO: "If you like our city, you'll love our suburbs."

WHERE YOU'LL LIVE AFTER ONE MONTH'S RENT RENDERS YOU HOMELESS: Aurora

Real-World city:
BOSTON

TYPICAL RESIDENT: student; professor

MAJOR ATTRACTION: clean subways, easily hopped turnstiles

MAJOR DETRACTION: plaid pants

POSTCOLLEGIATE PASTIME: graduate school

OFFICIAL CITY MOTTO: "Can I see some ID?"

WHERE YOU'LL LIVE AFTER ONE MONTH'S RENT RENDERS YOU HOMELESS: Somerville

Real-World city:
LOS ANGELES

TYPICAL RESIDENT: Evian-clutching actor-director-producer who is really tap water–clutching bartender-waitperson-baby-sitter

MAJOR ATTRACTION: gaining fame and fortune

MAJOR DETRACTION: losing pride

POSTCOLLEGIATE PASTIME: doing lunch

OFFICIAL CITY MOTTO: "We look *fabulous*."

WHERE YOU'LL LIVE AFTER ONE MONTH'S RENT RENDERS YOU HOMELESS: car

3 The majority of Real-World city residents must not live off trust funds.

4 There must be a minimum of 3 places to find a decent bagel in a Real-World city.

REAL WORLD

Real-World city:
WASHINGTON, D.C.

TYPICAL RESIDENT: **bitter public-interest lawyer; disillusioned lobbyist**

MAJOR ATTRACTION: **potential to run country**

MAJOR DETRACTION: **likelihood that you will**

POSTCOLLEGIATE PASTIME: **trying to explain your job to others**

OFFICIAL CITY MOTTO: **"Honk if you were a poli-sci major."**

WHERE YOU'LL LIVE AFTER ONE MONTH'S RENT RENDERS YOU HOMELESS: **Arlington**

Real-World city:
SAN FRANCISCO

TYPICAL RESIDENT: **mountain biker with a business plan**

MAJOR ATTRACTION: **pad thai**

MAJOR DETRACTION: **threat of plunging into earth's core**

POSTCOLLEGIATE PASTIME: **cross-dressing**

OFFICIAL CITY MOTTO: **"The weather was great until you got here."**

WHERE YOU'LL LIVE AFTER ONE MONTH'S RENT RENDERS YOU HOMELESS: **Oakland**

Real-World city:
DALLAS

TYPICAL RESIDENT: **cosmetically reconstructed ranchhand in $800 Ralph Lauren bolo tie**

MAJOR ATTRACTION: **air-conditioning**

MAJOR DETRACTION: **achy-breaky dancing**

POSTCOLLEGIATE PASTIME: **riflery; step class**

OFFICIAL CITY MOTTO: **"Charge it, cowboy."**

WHERE YOU'LL LIVE AFTER ONE MONTH'S RENT RENDERS YOU HOMELESS: **Garland**

SLACKER CITIES: LIVING IN THE UNREAL WORLD

If, through some glaring personal inadequacy, you have not mapped out your entire future by the time you've graduated, consider settling in one of the communities at right. Designed for those who wish to delay entry into the Real World indefinitely, each setting is ideal for the postcollegiate procrastinator who favors a job over a career, a Baggie full of homegrown pharmaceuticals over an HMO.

1. Telluride, CO
2. Madison, WI
3. Burlington, VT
4. Portland, OR
5. Austin, TX
6. Santa Cruz, CA
7. Boulder, CO
8. Sedona, AZ
9. Northampton, MA
10. Prague, CZ

REAL-WORLD MAP

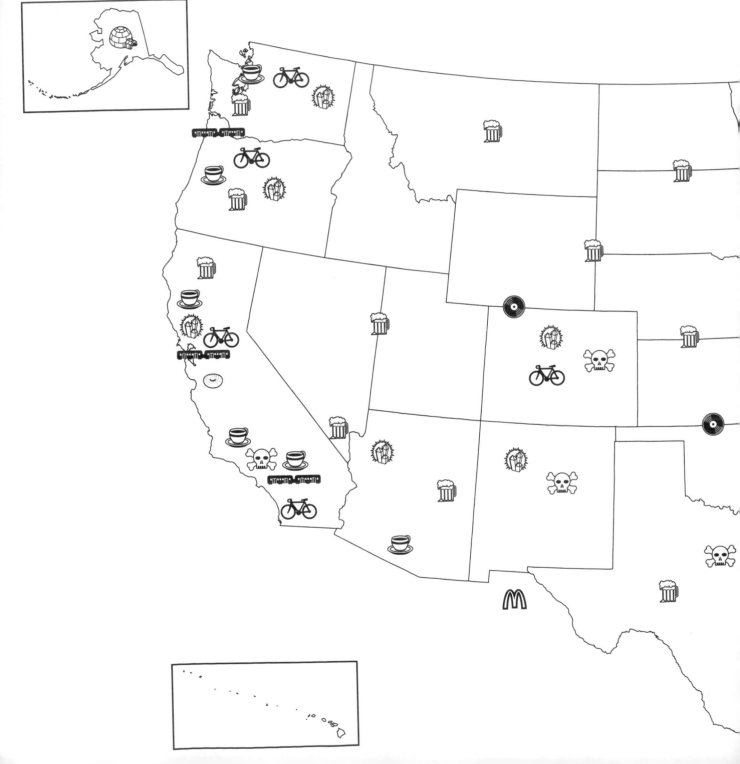

Still uncertain where to settle? The following map details the most important considerations nationwide. To find out which region is best for you, hang map on wall and follow these simple instructions:[2] **(A)** *Close eyes.* **(B)** *Throw dart.* **(C)** *Go.*

KEY:

🍺 = cheap beer region

⦿ = classic hits region

☕ = proliferation of caffeine

💎 = New Agers

○ = good bagels available

☠ = glut of baby boomers

🚲 = bike lanes

🚊 = good public transportation

Ⓜ = employment opportunities

▤ = high starting salaries

⛄ = affordable housing

[2] *alternate option: proceed directly to page 20.*

FROM DORM TO

Once you've settled on a city, the next step is finding a place to hang your hat. But first, you should find an apartment. Ideally, you will want one with such amenities as roof, walls, and floor, though you may have to settle for something affordable. Still, do not settle for the first dump you see. Look at many dumps, and, in time, you will find that special dump that suits your needs. That is because the more you look, the fewer needs you'll realize you have.

DUMP

LOCATION, LOCATION, LOCATION The three most important words in real estate are: "videorentalstore," "liquorstore," and "conveniencestore."

THE TWO MOST IMPORTANT WORDS IN REAL ESTATE The two most important words in real estate are: "rent control."

A rent-controlled apartment building is one in which the landlord is required to maintain more reasonably outrageous rents for the financially challenged, such as Entry-Level Lifers who are raking in ten grand a year picking up dry cleaning for their bosses. If you are lucky enough to live in one of the few cities that still provides this option, it just might be your ticket out of the projects.

You'll recognize a rent-controlled building by the disproportionate number of turbo Saabs in the parking lot. That is because in the Real World, rent control is for *Fortune* 500 CEOs, royalty, and anyone else with enough cash to pay the landlord off in exchange for lifelong low rent. It is no wonder, then, that rent-control residents tend never to die. On the off chance that one of them does indeed drop, an immediate relative or skilled impostor will be granted the apartment, and its accompanying gift of immortality.

But do not be discouraged from signing the waiting list for a rent-controlled building today. Then, once you are making a couple hundred grand, grab your checkbook, hop into your turbo Saab, and pay the landlord a return visit. Chances are, your name will miraculously jump right to the top of the list!

HOW TO FIND AN APARTMENT

As we have seen, it will be some time before you can afford rent control. But rest assured that several other options are open to the Entry-Level Lifer in search of shelter:

1 VISIT THE FRIENDLY REAL ESTATE AGENT. Bear in mind that the spacious, affordable apartments pictured in real estate agency windows do not exist in the Real World, and you're certain to find appropriately substandard housing with this method. Here's how: Upon expressing interest in one of the advertised apartments, you are befriended by a highly-coiffured individual with a diamond pinky ring and bad Binaca breath. After informing you that the apartment which lured you in "was just rented an hour ago," said individual begs to show you several "similarly priced" places that are "nearly identical." Reluctantly, you enter individual's white Trans Am and spend the afternoon looking at several "outrageously expensive" apartments that bear "no resemblance" to the one which lured you in. After calling 911 on the cellular phone, you should:

2 COMB THE CITY IN SEARCH OF ''FOR RENT'' SIGNS. The advantage to this approach is that it allows you to aimlessly wander around all day pretending to do something constructive instead of getting a job. But remember, most For Rent signs are displayed in apartment building windows mainly to prevent sleet from blowing in through the broken glass. It is also worth noting that no one ever answers the door to an apartment with a For Rent sign in the window. Except, of course, the urban cannibals who put them there to attract unsuspecting Entry-Level Lifers. That is why it is a far better idea to:

3 CAMP. An excellent alternative for the outdoorsy Lifer on a limited budget. Simply find your dream apartment building in the toniest part of town, pitch a tent in the parking lot, and place a decorative plastic flamingo outside to show your new neighbors you've arrived. With your impressive address, you'll be the envy of all your old college chums. After they've paid your vagrancy bail, you should:

4 EXAMINE FLYERS STAPLED TO TELEPHONE POLES. Ask yourself: "If this apartment is so great, why am I standing here reading a phone pole?" Besides, anyone with enough time on their hands to cut all those little notches into the bottom of the flyer, fill in their phone number twenty-seven times, and go around stapling it to telephone poles is the kind of person who is obviously avoiding necessary home repairs. You would be better off to:

5 CHECK THE CLASSIFIEDS. In addition to comics and TV listings, newspapers[3] contain classified advertisements for apartments. These are your best bet because someone actually paid money to place them, which shows they are not only desperate for renters, but can also read and write—skills worth holding out for in any landlord. More importantly, classifieds provide a valuable Real-World prop. Bring them to a smoky café where you can broodingly X out entire pages in display of your indubitable Real-Worldliness.

FOLLOWING UP

You never know when you'll get lucky enough to look at an apartment that bears a slight resemblance to its description in the classifieds, particularly if you are visually impaired. That is why it is important to follow up on every lead by calling the number listed and hanging up after an answering machine says, "If you are calling about the apartment, it has already been rented."

With persistence, you may get through to actual human beings—some with opposable thumbs—who will arrange times to show you the dwellings. Because these people have also agreed to meet other potential tenants—some

---

[3] *nonelectronic media available wherever you buy gum*

HOW TO DECIPHER A CLASSIFIED APARTMENT AD

Reading a classified ad for an apartment provides an excellent opportunity to utilize the foreign-language skills you would have learned in college had you attended class. Fortunately, mastering the language of the classifieds requires far less effort, and you will never be blindfolded and forced to bat wildly at a piñata. Consult the example at right for key words and phrases you'll need for fast fluency.

> FOR RENT: Stud. & czy, 2-bdrm apts. on 1st fl & PH of hstorc bldng on tree-lnd st. Kitchnt, W/D, exp brk wl & lots of charctr, incl. ww cpt, slpng lft, frplc. & skylt. Rent neg.

Translation:

STUDIO = Habitrail
COZY = suffocating
2-BEDROOM = one bedroom, closet
FIRST FLOOR = basement
PENTHOUSE = fourteenth-floor walk-up
HISTORIC = prehistoric
TREE-LINED STREET = unpaved road
KITCHENETTE = barbecue pit
W/D = walls/doors
EXPOSED BRICK WALL = what you see upon looking out window
CHARACTER = neglect

WALL-TO-WALL CARPETING = beautiful hardwood floors covered by 1973 orange, cat urine–scented shag rug
SLEEPING LOFT = torturous raised bed stage requiring victim to climb ladder, sleep with nose scraping against ceiling
FIREPLACE = lie
SKYLIGHT = roof leak
NEGOTIABLE = nonnegotiable[4]

[4] *exceptions for tenants insisting on paying more*

with actual sources of income—it is wise to drop frequent references to "my father the count" and "my mother the heiress." To secure the apartment, you must make a good impression.

HOW TO MAKE A GOOD IMPRESSION

THE SUCK-UP: One effective strategy is to suck up to the landlord in the same shameless manner that worked so well on your college organic chemistry professor. As you look around the apartment, make it perfectly clear that you love everything about it ("Light switches! I *love* light switches!"), and that you are the perfect tenant for the building ("I hope you're willing to accept the rent check long before the first of each month!"). The goal is to be so irresistible that the landlord will instantly turn the place over to you, give you the first month's rent free, and install ceiling fans.

THE BLOW-OFF: The other strategy is to feign indifference in the same shameless manner that worked so well on the object of your fourth-grade crush. If you love the bathroom, say, "I hate the bathroom." If the kitchen is twice the size of anything you've seen so far, say, "The kitchen is half the size of everything I've seen so far." The goal is to convince the landlord that you are a savvy customer who knows this apartment doesn't stand a chance of being rented—unless, of course, he or she is willing to instantly turn it over to you, give you the first month's rent free, and install ceiling fans.

THE COMPLETE ON-SITE INSPECTION

All too often, Entry-Level Lifers jump excitedly into the first apartment they can afford, neglecting to conduct a thorough inspection. One month later, they regret their decision to live on a toxic waste disposal site. This realistic scenario underscores the importance of carefully examining all potential residences. Make sure to pretend you know what you're doing in each case.

HOW TO EXAMINE THE APARTMENT

Upon entering the premises, complete these preliminary steps:

1. Measure something for no apparent reason.
2. Ask if heat is gas or oil, though you do not know what difference this makes.
3. Knock on some walls.
4. Frequently repeat the following phrase: "*hmmmmmmmmmm.*"

Having determined that the lodging is in satisfactory condition, you may proceed with the next and vastly more important steps:
5. Sleep over. Excellent way to evaluate decibel levels of neighbors' stereo/sex life/abused child.
6. Take shower on premises. Diagnostic test for dreaded freezing/scalding/freezing/scalding situation. Hint: If raw sewage does not come out of shower head, you cannot afford this apartment.
7. Invite friends over for rowdy "mock-housewarming party." If neighbors file police noise complaint, do not invite them to actual event upon moving in.
8. Place wheeled object on one side of kitchen floor. If apartment is slanted, object will roll to other side, and refrigerator will slam shut on your arm every time you open it.
9. Inspect upstairs neighbors' shoe collection. Cowboy boots, clogs, and/or high heels signal undesirable late-night stompers.
10. Set fire to building. Do smoke detectors sound? If not, replace batteries before moving in.

INSPECTION QUESTIONS. There are several important questions you must ask a landlord before considering any apartment. To avoid potential misunderstandings,[5] make sure you pose each question as specifically as possible. For example:

INSTEAD OF ASKING:	ASK:
Do you allow pets?	What would you do to my cat if you found out it was living here?
Are utilities included?	Are utilities available?
When will you raise the rent?	When will I be evicted?
Is this a good neighborhood?	What are all those hypodermic needles and broken glass vials doing in the hallway?
Why did the former tenants move?	What have you done with the former tenants?

[5] *e.g., you thought he said the place was free*

THE WINNING RENTAL APPLICATION

Once you have decided upon an apartment, you must complete a rental application designed to evaluate your prospects as a responsible, rent-paying tenant. Still, it need not destroy your chances of getting the apartment. Simply treat it the same way you did your college applications. Lie. Also, be sure to notify your friends that you've listed their numbers as references, though you've taken the liberty of upgrading their identities. Use this sample rental application as a model:

RENTAL APPLICATION FORM

name: Cecil/Mopsy (*insert one*) Rockefeller

occupation: Director of Funds Distribution, League of Philanthropic Tenants

salary: commensurate with prospective landlord's experience

present landlord and address: Trump, Donald; Trump Tower, NY, NY; 201-4823

reason for moving: finished paying for major home renovations that greatly increased landlord's property value at absolutely no expense to him

personal reference: Onassis, Jacqueline K.; 508-9963 (remind her you're calling about her Rockefeller friend's apartment)

in case of medical emergency, notify: Dr. C. Everett Koop; 415-4251

checking account (bank): First Bank of Zurich

savings account (bank): Geneva Savings and Loan

credit reference: Hearst, Uncle Bill; 617-0083

The reason you are having a hard time reading this part of the rental application is because it is known as the fine print, which few people ever actually read but everyone knows they should because it contains some very important information that, if magnified several thousand times and written in a language remotely resembling English, would amount to the fact that everything you've said above is true, which of course it is not, and although this offense is punishable by law, you are smart enough to realize that if you told the truth, you would never get this apartment, so go ahead and ignore this section completely, sign below, and start packing.

signature *Mopsy Rockefeller*

HOW TO SIGN THE LEASE

Because the lease is a legally binding document, be sure to act as though you understand it before signing. With it, you will be required to surrender first and last months' rent; a "finder's fee" if you used a real estate agency; a "payoff" if you went through a slumlord; your dignity; and a security deposit that will be returned to you later if the landlord (a) hasn't already spent it, and (b) somehow hasn't noticed the irreparable damage you have wrought upon his or her property.

Many Entry-Level Lifers have observed that the expenses involved in obtaining a lease would leave them eligible for food stamps. Therefore, these costs will have to be assumed either by your parents in the form of a guilt-induced loan, or by you in the form of a bouncing check. In the case of the latter, begin your search for another apartment immediately. You're about to learn that getting out of a legally binding document isn't so difficult after all!

A TENANT'S GUIDE TO THE LANDLORDS

At first, you may be secretly scared of the landlord you trick into giving you housing. After all, how many people do you know with the word "lord" in their title? Once you become more self-assured, however, you will realize that your initial fears were entirely justified. Landlords *are* one of the more frightening subspecies you will encounter in the Real World. The guide that follows will familiarize you with each strain:

THE DEMENTED OLD LADY:
- Several-thousand-year-old widowed Alzheimer's patient resembling "I've fallen and I can't get up" spokeswoman.
- Somehow accumulated prime real estate prior to losing all contact with reality; now rents for $18.99 per month.
- Never talks to you, though enjoys conversing with shrubbery and/or self.

THE SLUMLORD:
- Requires cash up front for privilege of illegally subletting tenement apartment.
- Says you can move in once he kicks out welfare mother, nine toddlers currently occupying unit.
- Makes monthly promise to put in window glass, remove indoor-outdoor carpet from living room.

THE NAÏVE NEWLYWEDS:
- Wretchedly perky yuppies who received two-family "investment" home as gift from parents.
- Spend entire weekend refinishing moldings in their unit; do not know how to fix toilet in yours.
- Decide to sell building as condo when maintenance starts cutting into golf time, allowing you two hours to move out.

MR./MS. FIX-IT:
- Recently retired carpenter-painter-plumber-electrician-exterminator; now fills days puttering around apartment conducting unnecessary repairs while whistling.
- Freely enters your apartment with master key while you are at work; in shower; having sex.
- Wrongly assumes that you possess a keen interest in diatribes concerning faulty wiring.

LANDLORD-AT-LARGE:
- Went underground immediately following lease-signing, never to be seen or heard from again.
- Requires rent checks made out to mysterious third party.
- Returns calls only after six-month rent strike; threatens eviction, goes back into hiding.

MEET YOUR NEIGHBORS

Though you may feel rather detached and melancholy the first few days in your new apartment, a host of friendly companions will soon be coming out of the woodwork.[6] As a gracious host, it is your duty to treat these guests with the kind of neighborly etiquette that ensures they will never return. Herewith, a primer on proper decorum:

Pop Quiz

ARE YOU LIVING IN THE REAL WORLD?

1. Men: Have you ever grown a beard or mustache?
2. Women: Have you experimented with at least three types of depilatories?
3. Men and women: Do you own a Gillette Sensor?
4. When you refer to "home," you mean:
(a) the home where you now live (b) the home where you grew up (c) the heating grate near the bus stop.
5. Have you ever purchased a paper-towel rack?

NEW NEIGHBOR	NEIGHBOR'S WELCOME GESTURE	PROPER DISPLAY OF GRATITUDE	PROTOCOL FOR UNEXPECTED VISITS
MR. MOUSE	leaves tiny gifts on kitchen table that definitely do not taste like peppercorns	wire trap, glue trap, D-Con poison pellets, steel wool–covered entrances, high-frequency device, cat	pour Drāno directly over neighbor, let stand overnight, dispose of neighbor's carcass
MR. COCKROACH	surprise party in sink	Black Flag spray, roach bomb, Combat traps, boric acid	deliver series of blows with boot heel until neighbor makes crunching noise
MRS. MOTH	free alterations of new clothing	mothballs, cedar blocks	stun neighbor in flight by spraying with Lemon Pledge
MR. ANT	helps clean up unsightly crumbs	Raid ant bait, Black Flag traps	using magnifying glass and light source, ignite neighbor
MR. AND MRS. JEHOVAH'S WITNESS	awaken you from Jagermeister-induced slumber by ringing buzzer thirty-seven times every Saturday morning	Doberman pinscher	see "Mr. Cockroach"

[6] *literally*

CREATING A HOUSEHOLD BUDGET:
THE NEGATIVE CASH FLOW PLAN

When planning household finances, experts recommend spending no more than twenty-five percent of your money on rent. This is good advice for Entry-Level Lifers wishing to live in Wauwatosa, Wisconsin. For others, balancing rent with living expenses requires more careful prioritizing. First, determine the percentage of your money that must go to "fixed" or "absolute" expenditures. Allocate the remaining percentages to low-priority, "secondary" expenses:

FIXED EXPENSES

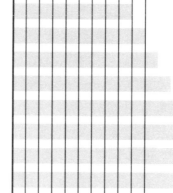

0 10 20 30 40 50 60 70 80 90 100

Rent-90%

Beer-100%

Chee•tos-110%

Entertainment (visual)-120%

Entertainment (audio)-130%

Entertainment (nonprescription)-140%

Entertainment (miscellaneous)-150%

Gap-200%

SECONDARY EXPENSES

0 10 20 30 40 50 60 70 80 90 100

Utility and phone bills-0%

Student loan bills-0%

Credit card bills-0%

Money owed to parents-0%

Money owed to friends-0%

Money owed to Lucky "The Horse" Gambini-0%

Car: insurance, parking violations, speeding tickets, maintenance-0%

Car: gas-0.1%

The Homecoming

It is not uncommon these days for many Entry-Level Lifers to temporarily move back in with Mom and/or Dad when they are feeling particularly masochistic, or simply intrigued by the idea of rent-free housing and a refrigerator stocked with edibles. These familial freeloaders have realized that reestablishing bonds with the folks after a lengthy absence makes sound financial sense. It could work for you, too, especially if you move your parents out first.

Certainly the biggest challenge of moving back home is identifying your former bedroom, which was transformed into some sort of multipurpose sewing room/study/guest bedroom/health club/wine cellar/walk-in closet/paper goods warehouse ten minutes after you first moved out. Once you've tracked it down, remove the tenant currently renting it. Next, treat yourself to a free imported beer and get reacquainted with your old stompin' grounds: the couch. Before long, you'll be right back in the swing of things: sleeping in and watching *I Dream of Jeannie* reruns while your parents are at work; making long-distance calls to all your nonmoving, nonshaking chums who were also humiliated into parental retreat; eating the dinners—complete with *salad*—your mother prepares for you when she gets back from work. Taking a little rest.

Most self-respecting parents have a threshold of about three weeks before the novelty of having you back home wears off and the horror that you might never leave sets in. They begin offering subtle updates on how successful all their friends' children have become. "The McGillicuddys' daughter just got promoted to *senior* associate assistant to the assistant," your mom mentions casually as you are trying to concentrate on the USA Network. "I heard Bernie Frumkin's boy landed the Dentu-Grip account over at the agency," your dad notes as you are staring off into space and picking your toes.

It won't be long before you're greeted each morning by a dozen want-ad sections from newspapers nationwide, each of which your mother has studied, demonstrating an uncanny knack for circling only those jobs which you'd be least interested in and most unqualified for. (*ATTENTION EMBOSSING-ENTHUSIASTS: HAVE YOU ALWAYS DREAMED OF A CAREER IN WHOLESALE STATIONERY DISTRIBUTION?*) You wonder: Is it just coincidental that all these positions are out of state? Your father, after a distinguished history of successful absentee-parenting, suddenly feels the need to guide and advise you—not with guidance and advice, but with photocopied *Business Week* articles about billionaire twenty-one-year-old entrepreneurs who do not live with their parents and do not eat Barney breakfast cereal for lunch.

You will know things are coming to a head the morning you return home from your first unexplained overnight absence. This is when you will discover, taped to your bedroom door, that first list of absurd chores. No mention of your disappearance will be made on this twelve-page document (after all, you are an adult now and are free to conduct your life on your own terms, according to Ann Landers), but it will be fairly clear from the nature of the tasks that Mom and Dad are out to regain some good old-fashioned control:

1. scrub inside fireplace
2. paint interior of garbage cans
3. remove dog droppings from lawn
4. sharpen all household scissors
5. clean decaying birds out of roof gutters
6. build addition onto kitchen
7. get job (often followed by passive-aggressive smiley face)

Should you ignore these arbitrary tasks designed to teach you the value of hard work (particularly number 7), your parents may employ several other strategies to get rid of you. They will force you to attend family functions. They will be on the phone outside your room and shout things like, *"No, Ralph, She Still Hasn't Started Looking For A Job Even Though She's Been Living With Us For Thirty-Seven Days Now!"* And, finally, they will resort to that most feared of all strategies: the "family discussion." Harsh words[7] will be exchanged. Years' worth of repressed anger will surface. Tears will be shed (particularly when they suggest that you start paying rent). Worst of all, you will miss the season finale of *America's Most Wanted.*

However, with open communication and mutual respect, all of these issues can be resolved by the modern dysfunctional family in a suitably rent-free fashion. That is why you must not make any hasty decisions about moving out until you are absolutely ready. How will you know when you are absolutely ready to move out? Follow this simple rule: The day you first realize you have picked up one or more of your parents' habits[8] is the day you are absolutely ready to move out. Don't waste any time. Go find yourself some *Real* roommates before it's too late.

---

[7] *"responsible"; "mature"; "career"*

[8] *especially: talking back to the television, developing an inability to focus a camera, and taking three hours to give car directions for a trip around the block*

ROOMMATES OF THE REAL WORLD

Unless you've always dreamed of living in a trailer park, you will most likely be splitting the rent on your first Real-World apartment with a roommate or two. Or seventeen. The good news is that you have vast prior experience living with others, thanks to those years you survived with college roommates, particularly the maniac from freshman year who listened to Wilson Phillips on *your* stereo. The bad news is that there's no Resident Assistant to run to anymore whenever your roomie overreacts about the food[9] you haven't yet cleaned off the floor. Fortunately, in the Real World, there are ways to ensure that you live with less fastidious individuals.

HOW TO FIND THE PERFECT ROOMMATE

Ideally, you will want to find someone with no prior arrest record. Failing that, you should find someone you know. Or at least someone who knows someone you know. Even if you can find someone who was once introduced to someone who knows someone you know, good enough. You know them. (As long as he or she isn't a Wilson Phillips fan.) But more likely, you will move to a city where the few people you know are already living with the few people they know. Worse, you will move to Boston, where everyone knows everyone, but you'd never want to live with them.

The following section offers three Real-World techniques for finding that perfect roommate. Do not spend too much time obsessing over which option is right for you.

Instead, take comfort in the knowledge that by the time you move out, you are going to hate your roommates no matter who they are.[10]

ROOMMATE ACQUISITION TECHNIQUE 1: FIND APARTMENT, SUBJECT OTHERS TO HUMILIATING SCREENING PROCESS.

This is by far the best choice for anyone who can counterfeit enough money to cover the first month's rent alone while searching for roommates. Not only does it enable you to snag the nice bedroom[11] and to decide who gets the less desirable one[12] down the hall, it also enables you to pose personal questions to a series of sociopaths you would never, under any circumstances, allow to live with you.

It is vital to conduct all roommate screenings in a mature and professional manner. Why not answer the door with a minicam strapped to your shoulder so you and your friends can later criticize each candidate's shortcomings during a private video retrospective? Also, you should require all aspiring roommates to submit a personal essay entitled "Why I Want to Live with You."[13] Finally, be sure to end every session with an "apartment-cleaning audition" to gauge how well each hopeful will perform if they get the part.

Of course, the most important aspect of any roommate screening is the interview itself. To find the perfect roommate, you must carefully construct a list of questions that provokes

---

[9] *regurgitated*
[10] *especially if they were once your best friends*

[11] *the one spacious enough to accommodate a dwarf-sized bed*
[12] *the one with bloodstains on the wall*
[13] *penmanship counts*

thoughtful, detailed responses and meaningful interactions in which both parties are left with lasting impressions of one another's true character. These probing questions are:

1. Do you own a VCR?

2. Do you own a CD player?

3. Do you own a microwave oven?

4. Do you own a remote-controlled TV?

5. Do you own a couch?

6. Do you now, or have you ever, owned a Wilson Phillips recording?

7. Do you enjoy working nights at the office and frequently sleeping over at your girl/ boyfriend's apartment?

8. Do you enjoy household chores?

9. Do you know anyone who can get me a job?

10. Do you have any contagious diseases?

ROOMMATE ACQUISITION TECHNIQUE 2: ANSWER ROOMMATE WANTED AD, SUBJECT SELF TO HUMILIATING SCREENING PROCESS. The advantage of this choice is convenience.[14] With all that MTV to watch, not to mention all those important job interviews to run to all day, it is far easier simply to answer an ad than to fill an empty apartment. And don't be concerned that you won't measure up to potential roommates' standards. All it takes is a quick glance at the Roommate Wanted advertisements to see that there are plenty of people out there searching for somebody just like you! Here is just one reassuring example:

ROOMMATE WANTED: Female seeks n-smkng, 23 ¾-yr.-old green-eyed, 5'2", curly-haired (auburn highlights) vegetarian of Indonesian ancestry. Prefer quiet trisexual harpsichordist/neurobiologist Democrat who voted Socialist in '92 & is skilled in refrigerator repair/papier mâché. No non-Mensas. Reply now—I'm flexible.

[14] *Remember this word.*

Once you've accumulated a lengthy list of possibilities, narrow it down to the one that includes a word or two about the actual room for rent. It would behoove you to be polite to the person who greets you at the door with a video camera and essay test, but until you are absolutely certain you want the apartment, be wary of anyone asking you to remove articles of clothing for the camera.

Remember, this is your opportunity to evaluate your potential home and the person(s) you'll be sharing it with. Instead of worrying whether you're providing all the right answers to their questions, ask a few of your own: "Have you ever had any problems fitting seventeen people into this studio?" "Why is that CONDEMNED sign hanging on the front door?" "What is that foul stench?"

It is also essential to snoop around the apartment when the residents are not looking. Flee the premises at once if you come across any of the following warning signs:

- stuffed animals
- handcuffs
- stuffed animals wearing handcuffs
- sink full of moldy plates
- pantry full of expensive china
- pet dressed in sweater
- *Soldier of Fortune* magazine
- *Good Housekeeping* magazine
- every foodstuff in refrigerator labeled with owner's name
- watercolors of cute kittens with heavily dilated pupils
- excessive Guatemalan handicrafts
- excessive use of potpourri
- feathered roach clip
- macramé wall-hangings
- glass menagerie collection

ROOMMATE ACQUISITION TECHNIQUE 3: SIGN UP WITH ROOMMATE-MATCHING SERVICE, HIT HUMILIATION JACKPOT. There are two things the Entry-Level Lifer needs to know about roommate services: (1) The people who sign up with them are looking for an apartment you cannot afford. (2) The people who sign up with them would not want to live with you anyway.

ANATOMY OF A REAL-WORLD ROOMMATE RELATIONSHIP
(INTERIOR: cramped postcollegiate apartment. It is 10 p.m. Both roommates have just returned from their nine-to-five jobs.)

FIRST ROOMMATE: Hi.
SECOND ROOMMATE: Hi.
FIRST ROOMMATE: How was your day?
SECOND ROOMMATE: Fine.
FIRST ROOMMATE: Good. Um . . . do you know whose turn it is to wash the dishes?
SECOND ROOMMATE: I think it's yours.
FIRST ROOMMATE: No it's not, you sniveling scum-sucker! I washed the dishes *last* time, and the time before that! You *never* wash the dishes, you lowlife shit-eating slob!

No matter how carefully you screen your roommates, it is important to remember that you will not make the right choice. In this section, we will assist you in identifying and eliminating the various individuals who will help make your home life miserable for the next few months.

THE PSYCHO FREAK

These deranged lunatics exhibit multiple personalities and unpredictable behavior, making them the ideal roommates for like-minded societal menaces. Each day with Psycho roommates brings a new surprise. Will they be sugary sweet or/and dangerously hostile to you? Will they emerge from their room at all? If so, will they be wearing your bathrobe again?

EARLY-WARNING SIGNS: The roommate candidate you like best during initial screenings is the probable Psycho. As a rule, they'll appear perfectly normal, intelligent, and friendly. This is because they are still on their medication, which they plan to discontinue once they move in with you.

Other telltale symptoms of the Psycho:

- refers to him/herself as "us"
- goes out for drink with "a friend," returns several weeks later
- never marks telephone calls to Bismarck, North Dakota, on bill though is only roommate whose entire circle of MCI family and friends lives in Bismarck, North Dakota
- your mother likes him/her

DOMESTIC DISPUTES: Psychos' inability to distinguish between "yours" and "mine" is the most commonly cited cause of attempted homicide by most normal roommates. Psychos have a tendency to adopt many of your possessions,[15] which you think you've misplaced un-

til one day you manage to short-circuit the security system they've rigged up to their bedroom and you discover your stereo; your bed; your grandfather.

Beyond being merely disturbed, Psychos are evil. Upon hearing your alarm clock each morning, they run to the bathroom to get in first. There, they help themselves to the last of the toilet paper, the last of the shampoo (yours), and the last of the razor blades, which they tend to use on arteries, not stubble. They take phone messages for you at their personal discretion, deciding for themselves whose call is or is not worth returning. They eat all of your frozen yogurt and put it back with one tablespoon (no nuts) left. Upon confrontation, they make *you* feel like the crazy one.

CONFLICT RESOLUTION:

- Perform exorcism.
- Perform ritual sacrificial killing.
- Move out.

THE ANAL-RETENTIVE

Though Anal-Retentives come in many varieties, a disproportionate number are employed in detail-oriented fields such as architecture, accounting, and computer science. If you suspect you've got one on your hands but aren't certain, ask yourself this question: Do you frequently leave something one way and return to find it another way? For example, have you recently put a glass down on the coffee table, left the room, and returned to find it drying in the drainboard? Has your entire CD collection ever been mysteriously alphabetized? If you answered "yes," slide a coaster under that mug before your roommate does, and read on.

EARLY-WARNING SIGNS: True to their namesakes, Anal-Retentives feel most at home in the bathroom, where they spend much of their time reorganizing the toilet paper roll so it pulls from under rather than over. It is also

[15] *including your personality*

common for Retentives to keep numerous colored plastic baskets neatly arranged on a Con-Tact paper–lined shelf, one filled entirely with cotton balls, another with Q-Tips, another with properly pH-balanced emollients, astringents, and cuticle-grooming implements. The area of the bathroom that has come to resemble a chemistry lab is actually the Retentive's contact lens caddy, where every ophthalmological device known to science is carefully laid out so that the Retentive may compulsively go about his or her mysterious daily lens rituals.

DOMESTIC DISPUTES: As you continue living with the Anal-Retentive, he or she will dispense with the oral tradition and begin leaving a steady stream of written correspondences on high-visibility areas like the answering machine, or your clothes. These begin harmlessly with reminders that it's your turn to take out the garbage or wash the dishes. Gradually, they get more detailed, culminating with elaborate freezer-defrosting, dishrag-ironing, and door-locking schedules, all written in the endearing first-person-plural style that goes something like, "Can we please remember when it is our turn to separate the recycling according to the numbers we see on the bottom of each item?"

Next, the financial spreadsheets appear, in which each roommate is given a column to record money spent on shared household items. At the end of the month, the Retentive, who has vigilantly recorded such purchases as *"1 package Post-it Notes @ .76 + .038 tax = .798,"* announces that he or she is owed several hundred dollars for the list of items purchased for shared consumption, none of which you either shared or consumed. You, on the other hand, have nothing written in your column except a fifty-cent pint of half-and-half you recorded the first week, before you decided this was too constipated an idea to continue.

CONFLICT RESOLUTION:

• Put Retentive's instincts to work for you by leaving out half-filled photo albums, shoeboxes full of unlabeled party tapes, your

blank 1040 individual income tax return, and anything that needs to be whipped into the Dewey Decimal System. Projects will be returned to you complete within twenty-four hours.

• Enjoy hearty laugh at Retentive's expense by secretly moving everything back the way it was prior to all Anal episodes.

• Move out.

THE ANIMAL

Nemesis of the Anal-Retentive, the Animal proudly boasts total disregard for basic human hygiene. It commonly marks its territory with a trail of rotting fruit, newspapers, and used tissues. Apparently raised by wolves, the Animal is also unaccustomed to such highly evolved skills as bathing, doing laundry, and eating with utensils.

EARLY-WARNING SIGNS: Many Animals give off a pungent odor to discourage interaction with higher life forms. They are a gaseous species that communicates in a language of lethal flatulence, endurance burps, and high-volume/maximum-resolution chewing. But perhaps the surest way to spot an Animal is to observe it hibernating in its natural environment, a bedroom festooned with soiled undergarments, empty beer cans, bowls of encrusted macaroni and cheese, and personal products that were meant to be disposed of after use.

DOMESTIC DISPUTES: Trouble starts when the Animal strays from its own breeding grounds to prey upon other areas of the apartment. Though you will try to train the beast by leaving notes around problem areas such as the kitchen (THANKS FOR NOT HACKING GIANT PHLEGM BALLS INTO SINK), it will be to no avail. The Animal will gradually infiltrate all areas of the apartment until you find yourself placing toilet paper on your own toilet seat before sitting down. Ultimately, the Animal begins attracting other forms of wildlife to the apartment, such as mice, cockroaches, and friends from high school.

CONFLICT RESOLUTION:

- Spay or neuter Animal to prevent reproduction.
- Install invisible electric fence around Animal's bedroom that delivers mild[16] shock upon crossing boundaries.
- Move out.

THE FORNICATOR

In the age of AIDS, many Entry-Level Lifers have chosen to limit sexual contact to just one partner. Unfortunately, the one partner they have all chosen is your roommate. You can probably hear him or her getting busy right now if you turn down the Megadeth you're blasting to drown out the even more disturbing sound of bedroom furniture about to crash through the ceiling. And perhaps you are asking yourself, "What does the Fornicator have that *I* don't have?" The answer, of course, is herpes simplex II.

EARLY-WARNING SIGNS: Upon snooping around the Fornicator's boudoir, many roommates have reported sightings of broken beds surrounded by candelabra, strange oils, startling arrays of contraceptive devices, a dog-eared *Joy of Sex*, fertility statuettes, kitchen ap-

pliances, a can of Reddi Wip, gardening tools, a gerbil, and many other lubricated objects. Also be on the lookout for mail-order literature in plain brown paper, and phone callers who inquire as to whether or not you are wearing underwear.

DOMESTIC DISPUTES: Problems arise when you are kept awake every night by moans, creaks, and occasional howls of livestock emanating from the Fornicator's room. Soon, the novelty of meeting new and naked strangers wandering around the apartment each morning wears off. Finally, when you are snuggled up on the living room couch one day and notice an odd new stain, you will become physically ill.

CONFLICT RESOLUTION:

- Identify job opportunity and launch lucrative prostitution ring from apartment.
- Drop subtle hints such as scrawling "For a good time, call . . ." on bathroom wall and/or installing deli-type ticket machine on Fornicator's door.
- Move out.

[16] *equivalent to voltage of standard electric chair*

. . . .

MORE FUN ROOMMATES

1. THE PARTY PERSON. *Using you as the subject of his/her personal sleep deprivation experiment, this wacky roommate enjoys inviting boisterous groups of alcoholics to gather outside your bedroom door each evening at 2 a.m. Typically employed in fields requiring nontraditional work schedules, such as waitperson, freelance artist, narcotics distributor.*

2. THE TALKER. *Born with no filter between brain and mouth, this roommate begins talking to you while you are taking your morning shower, continues while you are try-*

ing to read the comics at breakfast, and picks up where he/she left off as soon as you return from work. Enjoys asking questions during movies, repeating same story over and over, and greeting your friends with salutation, "Can you call back later? I'm on the other line."

3. THE PET. *This vicious cat, dog, rabbit, fish, and/or bird is vastly more important to your roommate than you will ever be, regardless of the fact that it relieves itself on your bed,* *feasts on your furniture, and acquaintance-rapes your leg.*

4. THE FOREIGNER. *This illegal alien was denied housing at the international graduate dorm but met your stringent roommate qualifications upon showing up at your door with American currency. Favorite phrases: "Very thank you," "I am sorry please," "Do not have cow, man!"*

5. THE COUPLE. *Because this roommate was initially disguised as a singular human being, you did not realize he or she came complete with a very significant other who would also be sleeping at your apartment, eating your food, getting hair in your shower*

drain, increasing your utility bills, receiving messages on your answering machine, and not paying rent.

6. THE HOMEBODY. *Having never set foot outside the apartment, this avowed agoraphobic considers you a guest in his/her home. Uncanny ability to be cooking when you* want *to cook, watching TV when you want to watch something else, occupying bathroom when you are on verge of bladder explosion. Bonus skill: makes you feel guilty when you leave premises to conduct outside life.*

7. THE ABSENTEE. *Never home, always pays. This is the roommate for you.*

· ·

A DUMP OF ONE'S OWN

In time, many Entry-Level Lifers end up living alone. This is because they have been convicted of premeditated murder and placed in solitary confinement. Or perhaps they have found an affordable apartment (otherwise known as "squatter's rights").

Most Lifers enjoy spending the first few weeks lounging in the comfort of their very own home. Soon they realize that their roommates had all the furniture and they have been lounging on a cold linoleum floor. This situation is easily remedied. Just be sure to keep copies of your old keys, and pay your former roommates a visit when you are sure they are not home. Bring a van so you can get everything in one trip.

Once you settle in, begin relishing your solitude. First, get a cat. If you're not a "cat person," a VCR is just as good. Also, you will need a decent phone since most of your solitude-relishing hours will be spent talking to others about how much you love being all by yourself.

If you get tired of calling in to all those talk-radio shows, another good way to relish your solitude is to have friends over for dinner seven nights a week so you never have to eat alone. These special visits enable you to engage in meaningful dialogue such as the following:

FRIEND: "Well, it's four a.m., I guess I should be going now."

YOU: "Oh you do, huh? Well, you're not going to get very far tied to that radiator."

Of course, the best part of living alone is that you no longer have to put up with slovenly roommates who never clean the bathroom or wash the dishes. Now you get to never do those things yourself, in the far more extravagant manner to which you've grown accustomed.

Pop Quiz

ARE YOU LIVING IN THE REAL WORLD?

1. Have you replaced your toothbrush in the past six months?
2. Have you ever brushed your teeth at work?
3. Have your parents recently begun confiding in you?
4. Do you apply any sort of cream to your face before going to bed at night?
5. Do you have more than four keys on your key chain?

How to Live in Sin

If you're like most Entry-Level Lifers, you've probably always worried that moving in with your girlfriend or boyfriend is one of those monumental decisions that must be based on mutual devotion, unbridled commitment, and levelheaded maturity. This couldn't be further from the truth. In the Real World, the decision to cohabit is based on more important considerations, such as if you split the cost of one dump rather than continue to pay for two, there will be money left over for HBO. Also, once you've both entered the world of nine-to-five,[17] the odds of occasionally running into each other are greater if you have the same address. If you are still uncertain whether you are ready to live together, ask yourself the following question: "If forced, would I be able to remember what my *own* apartment looks like?"

Another common mistake is to assume that living together is a trial before marriage.[18] This mistake is most often made by your parents, who are more familiar with trials *after* marriage. They may pretend they are "hep" and "with-it" when it comes to your "arrangement," but secretly they cannot stand the fact that you are postponing such a sacred tradition as matrimony. This is ironic coming from two people who were still in their cavity-prone years when they tied the knot. Don't make the same mistake. Wait to get married until you feel absolutely certain you need (a) kitchenware (b) a green card or (c) better health insurance to cover your new love-child.

Until then, cohabitation provides all the other advantages of the M word. Women: You'll wonder how you ever lived without such a thoughtful, considerate partner each and every time you sit down on a subarctic porcelain toilet bowl. Men: Imagine your arousal as you gaze longingly at your true love with mustache bleach on her lip. All this, *plus* you can have passionate premarital sex whenever you want, such as once every other week after *Seinfeld* and three alternating Saturday nights per month except during leap years.

Still, many Entry-Level Lifers want more of a commitment from cohabitation, yet aren't ready for marriage. It is with their edification in mind that we present the do-it-yourself . . .

LIVING IN SIN CEREMONY

(*Both Sinners remove Walkmen, turn to face each other:*)

FEMALE SINNER (to Male Sinner): Do you, what was your name again?—oh, yeah, *[insert name here]*, promise to have, hold, and operate the remote control like a normal human being, wash the dishes until such time as they are visibly cleaner, spend less than six hours per session in the bathroom reading magazines targeted at fourteen-year-olds, and never use pet names in public, especially Boo-Boo, Fuzzy, or Duck, for as long as we both shall be able to afford the rent?

MALE SINNER (to Female Sinner): I guess.

MALE SINNER (to Female Sinner): Do you, um, yeah—you in the mustache bleach—promize to learn how to operate the VCR, never mix my CDs with your CDs, prevent feminine hygiene products from taking over the apartment building, curb tendencies to drape hosiery on all available doorknobs, and never use pet names in public, especially Pooh-Bear, Sweetiecheeks, or Schmuck, for as long as we both shall be able to afford the rent?

FEMALE SINNER (to no one in particular): I guess.

You may now pronounce yourselves cohabitors. (*Sinners look into each other's Ray-Bans, exchange cubic zirconium rings, raise arms for meaningful high five, and sign lease.*)

17 *a.m.*

18 *a period of time immediately preceding divorce*

HOUSEHOLD CHORES

A PRACTICAL APPROACH. It is always prudent to divide household maintenance responsibilities evenly among all roommates so there is nothing left for you personally to maintain. The best idea is to call an apartment meeting and devise a detailed chart of each individual's obligations. Bear in mind that this chart will be ignored by all parties within seconds of the meeting's conclusion. At that time, you will want to consult the meticulously researched guide below:

Household Duty	Suggested Frequency	Whose Responsibility
1. dishwashing	whenever you have run out of clean dishes, bought new set, run out again	your roommates'
2. pet feeding	whenever Fluffy begins feeding on own appendages	your roommates'
3. dusting	upon first sighting of tumbleweed rolling through living room	your roommates'
4. food shopping	national holidays or other emergencies when take-out is unavailable	your roommates'
5. bathroom cleaning	when densely grown fungi make it impossible to observe sea creatures cavorting in toilet	your roommates'
6. taking out garbage	when refuse has fully decomposed	your roommates'
7. window washing	upon discovery that, no, it is not stained glass after all	your roommates'
8. floor washing	when mice stick directly to linoleum before reaching glue trap	your roommates'
9. bill-paying	first of every month in which you notice phone, electricity, heat, and apartment keys no longer seem to work	your roommates'
10. vacuuming	never	yours

INFERIOR DECORATING

When beautifying your first Real-World apartment, remember the term "transitional housing."[19] It would be folly to waste time trying to make it nice. If you want nice, go visit your parents' house. And don't forget to bring your laundry and confiscate a few butter knives while you're there.

The most effort you'll want to put into your new place is painting over the blinding shade of "landlord white" (or worse, "*aged* landlord white") it currently sports. But don't get too artsy. Primary colors are considered too artsy by most landlords. With a little convincing, however, he or she may throw caution to the wind and allow you to use a more daring shade of off-white. A whole variety of these dynamic hues is available at your local hardware store with names apparently coined by the author of the *Tweeds* catalog: Whispering Ivory Tusk; Morning Eggshell; Newborn Jaundice.

Whichever shade of off-white you choose, do not attempt to paint the apartment by yourself. Instead, manipulate friends into doing it by inviting them to a painting *party* at which you provide plenty of free beer and Smartfood so they think they're having fun instead of doing manual labor. Frighteningly, you will discover that some friends seem to enjoy paint-

[19] *definition: If there is a God, you will not live here more than a year.*

ing your apartment, and even come equipped with their own personal edging and rolling devices. Be nice to these people. They will come in handy at a later date.

As for those with less steady hands—the ones who manage to squeegee down live insects and paint over previously transparent windows—engage them in a separate party game. A traditional Real-World favorite is "Moving Company," in which players haul your heaviest and most carelessly packed possessions up twelve flights of stairs before being rushed to the emergency room.

CURBSIDE FURNISHING It's no mistake that the minimalist look is a classic among Entry-Level Lifers who've decided that regular meals are more important than a matching living room set. Stark blank walls, maybe a pillow on the floor. Very Zen. But did you know it is possible to fill your estate with actual *furniture* for free? It's true, if you know how to shop.

We're talking, of course, about garbage picking. City streets become furniture showrooms of the great outdoors each evening prior to trash collection day. Go hunting and gathering in the right part of town, and you never know what you'll come home with: weird and enormous spools of rotting wood (coffee tables!); moldy shower curtains (drapes!); dog-chewed chunks of foam rubber (a bed!). You might even find some preassembled furniture such as shiny Formica dressers and Naugahyde beanbag chairs. And for the walls, such *objets d'art* as melancholy clown portraits painted on genuine velveteen canvas.

But why stop there? While you're at it, you may as well drag home a few actual garbage cans (food storage!) to add the finishing touches to your stylish new spread.

FURTHER ADVENTURES IN FURNITURE
Having established that furniture is often mistakenly identified as garbage, we move on to an equally important lesson: Garbage is often mistakenly identified as furniture. Where can the Entry-Level Lifer acquire such refuse? There are several options:

I. GARAGE SALES. People who sell their furniture at garage sales have finally decided that it is too old, too ugly, and too uncomfortable to suit their needs. Why not seize the opportunity to suit *yours*? When attending a garage sale, avoid arriving too early in hopes of scooping up that larvae-contaminated couch before another shrewd Lifer beats you to it. Instead, arrive late, when desperate garage sellers would peddle their own children for a fast couple of bucks. Better yet, forget the sale altogether and come back on trash-collection day when the same furniture will be available for free.

II. PARENTS' ATTIC. If the idea of sleeping on the bed in which you were conceived does not induce nightmares or insomnia, there is an important item of furniture awaiting you in your parents' attic. Here, among the other debris set aside for the alleged garage sale they have been planning since the turn of the century, you will find several generations of furnishings your folks have completely forgotten about. It is a good idea to sneak these out while they are away, however, taking into consideration their delusions that whatever *is* up there must be very valuable.

If you are lucky enough to be the product of a broken home, you might even find something relatively modern among the ruins, such as that Lucite living room set your dad's second wife made him replace as soon as she turned twenty-one.

III. SALVATION ARMY. It is unclear from historical documentation which war the Salvation Army fought, but it is apparent from their spoils that they won. Army headquarters overflow with used furnishings of the same civilian quality one would expect to find elsewhere, such as at the local landfill. The main concern for shoppers is not quality, but morality: In this age of decreased defense spending, do you really want your furniture dollars going into the pockets of the military? More importantly, is that kitchen table really going to fit through your door?

1. file cabinet

2. closet

3. chair

4. pet cage

5. coffee table

MILK CRATE

It's three a.m. Furtively, you sneak around to the "deliveries only" section of the grocery store parking lot. That's where you spot them, glowing in the moonlight like a stack of indestructible plastic gifts sent down from the heavens. You remove your stocking mask for a closer look. The coast is clear. You act, swiftly and courageously, tearing off into the night with your priceless new possessions.

6. bookshelf

7. catcher's mask

8. storage of old albums

9. storage of old everything

10. storage of milk

REAL-WORLD DECORATING
DOS AND DON'TS

1. DO remove clear plastic slipcovers from furniture inherited from dead grandparents. Being nonperishable, upholstery does not require storage in Saran Wrap.

2. DON'T place Christmas lights anywhere other than on a large evergreen tree during the month of December. You live in an apartment building, not Santa's workshop.

3. DO paint directly over simulated wood paneling and visually offensive wallpaper. (For color options, see page 29.)

4. DON'T stack beer cans in pyramid formation on windowsill. Stack in shopping bag and return for money.

5. DO place mattress at least two feet off floor. It will prevent rodents from crawling in with you.

6. DON'T succumb to inexplicable urges to buy weird wicker furniture from Pier 1 Imports. Wicker is best reserved for weaving baskets and feeding farm animals.

7. DO install curtains or blinds. They are more aesthetically pleasing than the plywood boards currently nailed to your windows.

8. DON'T introduce anything onto the premises preceded by the word "*faux*." It is cheaper to stick with the genuinely fake stuff.

9. DON'T hang up unicorn posters with trite sayings on them. "If you love something, tear it off the wall and rip it to shreds."

10. DON'T drape Indian print tapestries from the ceiling. They will only absorb the leak and drip on the Indian print tapestries draped over the couch.

A RENTER'S CHECKLIST

Contrary to what the window dressers at Conran's would have you believe, there are really only a handful of items the Entry-Level Lifer needs to live comfortably. Herewith, the essentials:

 ○ TV

 ○ Round rice-paper light fixture

 ○ diseased ficus plant

 ○ map of place you can't afford to visit

 ○ cinder blocks

 ○ wooden box for cassettes

 ○ TV

 ○ 500 extension cords

 ○ milk crates

 ○ answering machine

 ○ lumpy futon

 ○ TV

EVOLUTION OF THE LIVING ROOM

FIGURE A

FIGURE B

REAL-WORLD MEAL PLANS

To meet your changing nutritional needs as you make that delicate dietary transition into Entry-Level Life, it will be necessary to modify the four college food groups: beer, grilled cheese, Snickers, and bad cafeteria coffee. For optimum performance, it is time you began eating a balanced diet from the four Real-World food groups. These are:

1. TAKE-OUT. This food group provides Chinese, pizza, Mexican, burger, California roll, McNugget and other important nuggets and minerals necessary for digestive difficulties.

2. DELIVERY. This food group is fortified with all the nutritional benefits of group 1 with no additional energy expenditure.

3. VENDING MACHINE. This food group provides the recommended daily allowance of Diet Coke and stale Pepperidge Farm goldfish.

4. RESTAURANT. This food group provides you with essential employment opportunities.

SMART SHOPPING

One of the best parts of Entry-Level Life is that you will never again stand in long lines at the cafeteria, only to leave hungry in search of something found on the food chain. Now you get to stand in infinitely longer lines at the supermarket, where you can shamelessly catch up on the latest Elvis/UFO/dog-faced boy sightings in *Weekly World News*. You may also want to buy some food while you are there.

Many Entry-Level Lifers have described exciting sensations of adulthood and maturity upon first-time grocery experiences, particularly as they stride down the aisles pushing sleek chrome carts they were once forced to straddle by abusive mothers. This feeling usually subsides when they realize that they are now pushing their roommates around in the cart. To prevent similarly regressive behavior,

especially Silly String—like encounters in the Cheez Whiz aisle, it is a good idea to leave your roommates home when food shopping. This will also prevent public bloodshed among roommates who cannot agree on such complex choices as white/wheat/oat, skim/whole/2%, and chunky/extra-chunky/smooth.

Finally, do not be embarrassed if you binge the first few times you go shopping, and bring home enough food to feed Somalia. In time, you'll be able to find the "one item or less" checkout lane blindfolded.

To get the most out of your grocery-shopping spree, remember these "Smart Shopping Tips":

SMART SHOPPING TIP #1: Proceed Immediately to Frozen Foods Aisle. The most important section of any grocery store contains the fundamentals of a balanced Entry-Level meal: microwave dinners and Heath Bar Crunch.

SMART SHOPPING TIP #2: Buy Generic Everything.[20] Generic products are equally inferior to brand-name merchandise, and often more reasonably overpriced.

SMART SHOPPING TIP #3: Try Before You Buy.[21] This moneysaving device is most easily employed on weekend afternoons when overly enthusiastic cheese and juice representatives put their goods out for public consumption. For a less vile alternative, try foodstuffs on shelves, making sure to replace unchewed portions for other consumers.

SMART SHOPPING TIP #4: Read Labels Carefully. Choose only products containing triethylxanthiumgl and other lethal, nonpronounceable preservatives that allow your food to fossilize properly once you've forgotten about it in the far reaches of your refrigerator.

[20] *except toilet paper*
[21] *except toilet paper*

Pop Quiz

ARE YOU LIVING IN THE REAL WORLD?

1. Have you ever sent a floral arrangement?
2. Have you ever bought flowers for your apartment?
3. Have you recently caught yourself yawning aloud in a public place?
4. Have you ever attended a nighttime party where a child was present?
5. Do you make your bed?

SMART SHOPPING TIP #5: Stop Clipping Coupons. (*a*) You never remember to bring them to the store. (*b*) When you do remember to bring them to the store, you forget to give them to the cashier. (*c*) When you don't forget to give them to the cashier, you do forget that superabsorbent Pampers, pimento loaf, and matzoh meal are items you did not need just because you had the coupons.[22]

SMART SHOPPING TIP #6: Think Jumbo Size. Purchasing items in eighty-packs and institutional-size vats ensures that there will be leftovers after roommates secretly consume your food.

THE JOY OF NOT COOKING

1. How to cook turkey

3. How to cook seafood

2. How to cook rack of lamb

4. How to cook herb roasted chicken with gravy with white and wild rice, broccoli florets, carrots with butter sauce, and cherry crisp dessert

[22] *especially since the coupons expired several years ago*

THE NO-NUKES PLAN: ENTRY-LEVEL RECIPES FOR DISASTER

Shockingly, there remains a small contingency of Entry-Level Lifers who are more concerned about gene mutation than high-velocity cooking. This is usually because they were not fortunate enough to be raised in nuclear families, those in which both mother and father live at the office and teach children the value of a hearty, home-nuked meal early on. Here, we offer several tempting dishes for those who prefer their repasts radiation-free.

REAL-WORLD RECIPE #1:

STIR FRY SURPRISE

What you'll need:

-entire contents of refrigerator and pantry

-soy sauce

-wine

Preparation:

1. Empty entire contents of refrigerator and pantry into large frying pan.[23]
2. Add soy sauce.
3. Add wine.
4. Add more wine.
5. Stir.
6. Fry.

Yield: several fistfuls

REAL-WORLD RECIPE #2:

SAME OLD SPAGHETTI

What you'll need:

-same spaghetti you've eaten every night this week

-ketchup

-wine

Preparation:

1. Remove desired amount of spaghetti from box.
2. Place approx. ½ back inside because you've removed too much.
3. Place spaghetti in pot of water on high heat. Cover.
4. When lid is forced off by foam geyser, remove from heat.
5. Drain any remaining traces of water.
6. Add ketchup.
7. Add wine.
8. Add more wine.

Yield: too much

[23] *may substitute still-unopened wok received as graduation gift from New Age uncle*

REAL-WORLD RECIPE #3:

RAMEN NOODLES

What you'll need:

-some food

-wine

Preparation:

1. Pour boiling water into styrofoam cup containing what appears to be freeze-dried space food.
2. Pour generous glass of wine.
3. Try to find "Ramen" on map of world.
4. Call Domino's.

Yield: one cold pizza

REAL-WORLD RECIPE #4:

BANANA

What you'll need:

-banana

-bourbon

Preparation

1. Peel and eat banana while running frantically to catch subway you will miss, causing you to be late for most important meeting of the year.
2. Wash down with bourbon to eliminate traces of banana breath.
3. Wash down with more bourbon to eliminate traces of sobriety.

Yield: one termination-of-employment notification

CO-OP COOKING: JUST SAY NO

Avoid those fascist households where residents insist upon preparing and eating all meals together in tiresome efforts to "think globally, act locally." These humorless eating environments do nothing to enhance your status as an Entry-Level Lifer. Instead, they hark back to your pre-Real-Worldly days, when it is not entirely beyond the realm of possibility that you had *time* for such tomfoolery. Now, after a hard day's work, you will much prefer to come home, nuke yourself a Lean Cuisine, and enjoy your meal alone[24] as you reflect upon the day's many accomplishments. The last thing you'll want to do is cook for a house full of patchouli-soaked macrobiotics who aren't happy until everyone has been served equal portions of tofu lasagna.

Of course it is nice to have a meal with your roommates every now and again. But in the Real World, these things are best done in expensive restaurants when parents come to town with credit cards.

[24]*or with Alex Trebek*

SECTION II

Entry-Level Job Hunt

CRASH-
LANDING
A JOB

FREEDOM OVERLOAD. In the olden days, choosing an occupation was a simple matter of going out and finding any backbreaking labor that would put food on the table. Things are no longer so cushy. In today's Real working World, not only are you saddled with a dizzying array of professional possibilities, you must also spend countless fatiguing hours contemplating which will be the most personally rewarding and professionally enriching.

Thus burdened, many Pre-Employed Lifers develop the debilitating symptoms of Freedom Overload. One moment they plan to become a certified public accountant, the next they are going to move to Utah and breed llamas. This week they are certain they want to be a rabbi, next week they are interviewing for the job of dental hygienist.

The solution is to select an occupation the same way you selected your college courses: according to which ones start latest in the afternoon. Unfortunately, most bartending jobs now require advanced degrees. Be prepared to fall into a more professional, lower-paying "career" first.

Should you have any further career-related concerns, consult the guide below. It contains some reassuring answers that will make falling into a career as easy as falling off a cliff.

COMMON PRELIMINARY JOB-HUNTING QUESTIONS

Q) In the Real working World, does my college GPA matter?
A) No.

Q) In the Real working World, does my college major matter?
A) No.

Q) In the Real working World, does the fact that I did not graduate from an Ivy League college matter?
A) No.

Q) In the Real working World, does the fact that I did not actually graduate from college at all matter?
A) Not unless your parents find out.

WHAT COLOR IS YOUR STRAITJACKET?

Traditional wisdom dictates that before embarking on a job search, you must perform an exhaustive battery of self-assessment exercises to find your hidden skills and talents. The most common result is discovering that you have none. If you were skilled and talented at finding a job, you would be out looking for one instead of sitting around in your underwear performing an exhaustive battery of self-assessment exercises.

Many Pre-Employed Lifers begin with the career aptitude quizzes in the stunningly incomprehensible book *What Color Is Your Parachute?* Because they do not even understand the question posed by the book's title, however, they do not get very far in their careers.

The self-assessment exercises below serve the same purpose as those in books disguised as skydiving manuals. First of all, they provide an excellent way to waste time. More importantly, they give you the false sense of confidence you'll need to get out into that job market and compete without a shred of prior experience.

EXERCISE IN FUTILITY #1:

Pretending You Are Not Completely Unemployable

This exercise is designed to make you feel as if you have many of the characteristics employers look for in qualified job candidates. First, get a sheet of scrap paper. Got one? Splendid! By getting a piece of scrap paper, you've demonstrated the kind of resourcefulness that any employer would consider an enormous asset. It won't be long now before you land that job!

On the left side of the page, make a list of the professional attributes you would possess if you were someone who had a shred of prior experience. On the right side, fill in something you have done in the past that illustrates each of these attributes. When you are finished, you will see for yourself that you have all the "right stuff." Here's how a typical chart will look:

PROFESSIONAL ATTRIBUTE	DEMONSTRATED ABILITY
Resourcefulness	*How I got that piece of scrap paper.*
Leadership	*I led our dog on walks before it got put to sleep.*
Working Well With Others	*That time junior year when I copied the statistics final off the girl who sat next to me AND the guy in front of me.*
Quick Learner	*I learned to breathe through mouth on first try.*
Effective Communicator	*That time I talked to Pat on the phone for 17 hours straight.*
Organizational Ability	*I have one of those stackable plastic holders that organizes my sweaters in one part and my shirts in another part.*
Good Problem Solver	*How I always say, "No problem."*

EXERCISE IN FUTILITY #2:

Pretending That "If You Do What You Love, The Money Will Follow"

Certainly, this aphorism holds true for anyone who loves to sneak up on senior citizens, kick their walkers right out from under them, throw them to the ground, and take all their money. But what about *you*? What do *you* love to do? Compose a list of the many interests, passions, and talents you have that can be channeled into a lucrative career.

EXERCISE IN FUTILITY #3:

Pretending That Everything Will Be Okay Even Though You Left Exercise #2 Blank

To satisfactorily complete this exercise, you need only answer the simple questions below:

Vocational Aptitude Survey

Do you like to travel?
THEN YOU SHOULD BE A: *cab driver*

Do you enjoy close physical contact with children?
THEN YOU SHOULD BE A: *priest*

Do you enjoy being outdoors?
THEN YOU SHOULD BE A: *prostitute*

Do you enjoy prostitution?
THEN YOU SHOULD BE AN: *advertising copywriter*

Do you like working with mentally challenged adults?
THEN YOU SHOULD BE A: *television producer*

Do you like working with wild animals?
THEN YOU SHOULD BE A: *commodities trader*

Are you good with numbers?
THEN YOU SHOULD BE A: *directory assistance operator*

Do you like politics?
THEN YOU SHOULD BE AN: *office worker*

Do you enjoy working with your hands?
THEN YOU SHOULD BE A: *gynecologist*

Do you want to dedicate your life to making change?
THEN YOU SHOULD BE A: *cashier*

Do you enjoy cleaning up the environment?
THEN YOU SHOULD BE A: *garbage collector*

Would you like to risk your life in the line of duty?
THEN YOU SHOULD BE A: *drivers' ed. instructor*

Are you misanthropic?
THEN YOU SHOULD BE A: *customer service representative*

Do you enjoy watching daytime television?
THEN YOU SHOULD BE A: *free-lancer*

Do you like nonprofit work?
THEN YOU SHOULD BE AN: *entry-level employee of a multibillion-dollar corporation*

Pop Quiz

ARE YOU LIVING IN THE REAL WORLD?

1. Are you best friends with someone you hated in high school?
2. Do you hate someone you were best friends with in high school?
3. Have you ever been to a bed-and-breakfast?
4. Do you own three or more items of Tupperware?
5. Have you recently discovered Books on Tape?

HOW TO FAKE A RÉSUMÉ

In the Real working World, you can be anyone you want to be. All you need is a fraudulent résumé. On a single page, you must show prospective employers that you are a skilled, well-rounded, highly experienced professional. One idea is to send someone else's résumé. But you won't be fooling anyone. Employers know very well that you are just another bachelor or bachelorette of arts who has spent the last twenty-odd years in[1] school. What they want to know from your résumé is whether you've learned anything that will be useful in the Real working World.

Show them that you have. Send them an obviously deceitful, conspicuously dishonest version of your *own* résumé. You will stand out as a candidate with great promise.

HOW TO DESIGN YOUR RÉSUMÉ

First, identify a résumé-obsessed friend with access to a Mac and laser printer. Then casually ask for advice: "My, you seem to know a lot about résumés," you might begin in the way of cheap flattery. "In your estimable opinion, should I put my address in boldface or italics?"

[1] *or around*

This question will normally be met with alarming fervor:

"*Italics!* Definitely! I've got twenty-seven different books on résumés and every one of them says you've *got* to italicize or you won't get the job! And you've *got* to skip an inch and three-eighths between your name and address and boldface your career objective or they're going to throw it away *immediately!* Look, do you want me to do your résumé for you?"

At this point, hand your friend the rough draft in your back pocket. Do not worry that it is written on a paper napkin still damp from the Bloody Mary you spilled on it this morning. It is your friend's responsibility to make it look better.

CREATIVE WRITING YOUR RÉSUMÉ

Freed from the chore of creating a favorable appearance for your résumé, refocus your energy on creating a favorable appearance for *yourself.* This is not as impossible as it may appear. Simply remember three words:

1. FABRICATE
2. EXAGGERATE
3. LIAISON

1 FABRICATE the kinds of jobs that make your résumé stand out over all others. What about that time you were elected President of the United States? That is exactly the sort of job that shows you are a good manager. Do not worry that anyone will check your references—it's nearly impossible to get through to the White House.

2 EXAGGERATE your importance in every job you claim to have held. Using a thesaurus,[2] invent job titles that reflect your indispensable role in each organization. For example, which of the following job titles describes the role you played the day you filed invoices at your mother's office? (a) Filer or (b) Principal Alphabetizing Coordination Systems Technician Specialist. If you thought choice "a" was more accurate, you were right! Therefore, proceed with choice "b."

After your job title, include a brief yet highly **exaggerated** description of the specific duties you performed in each position. This is done by using "résumé words."

Pop Quiz

ARE YOU LIVING IN THE REAL WORLD?

1. Are you now or have you ever been addicted to Carmax?
2. Do you have a "morning routine"?
3. Have you accumulated more than 2,000 miles on any one frequent flier program?
4. Do you own a vegetable peeler?
5. Do you recognize the person pictured above your name in your high school yearbook?

EXAMPLES OF RÉSUMÉ WORDS

· implemented	· prepared
· coordinated	· conducted
· provided support for	· applied
	· presented
· managed	· evaluated
· assisted	· assessed
· led	· supervised
· administrated	· organized
· initiated	· executed
· participated	· performed
· gathered	· integrated
· directed	

Be specific with your job descriptions. Don't just tell employers you "implemented," tell

them exactly how *much* you implemented. Don't tell them you "executed," tell them how *many* people you executed. To be specific, insert plenty of "résumé numbers."

EXAMPLES OF RÉSUMÉ NUMBERS

· millions	· many, many, many
· billions	
· trillions and trillions	· scores
	· scads
· quadrillions	· reams
· many	· truckloads
· many, many	· too numerous to mention

3 ACT AS A LIAISON in each and every job you dream up. Do not be distressed if you don't know what a "liaison" actually is. Here is the definition according to the dictionary:[3] *liaison: "an illicit sexual relationship; an affair."* When you emphasize your vast professional experience in this area, your chance of being called in for an interview is nothing less than guaranteed.

As you set forth to fabricate, exaggerate, and act as a liaison, be sure not to overlook the other key elements of your Entry-Level résumé:

I. NAME: In today's global economy, the best jobs will go to those with international experience and a mastery of the multicultural marketplace. You can become one of these people by properly wording the "name" component of your résumé. For instance, suppose you spot a position calling for an omnilingual native of Guadalajara, Mexico, who has twenty to thirty years' experience as an English translator at the Canadian Embassy in Bogotá, Colombia. If you do not have a Hispanic name, simply use the one your freshman Spanish teacher gave you. Here are some examples of appropriate résumé names:

---

[2] *computerized euphemism-finder available with "spellcheck" on many word processing systems*

[3] *look it up*

Si tu nombre es:	En el Mundo Real, tu nombre es:
Steve	Esteban
Bob	Roberto
Lisa	Luisa
Phil	Felipe
Nancy	Nancy

II. CAREER OBJECTIVE: Do not be self-centered with your career objective. Select one that shows you are selflessly concerned with your potential *employer's* career objective:

Career Objective: An entry-level position allowing me to utilize my skills of making an obscene amount of money for my potential employer.

See how easy this can be when you get right to the heart of the issue at hand?

III. EDUCATION: To save space, list only the most prestigious institutions—including any you may have attended. Be sure to include the many awards and honors you have bestowed upon yourself.

IV. ACTIVITIES: This section of your résumé should give the illusion that you are a fascinating and well-rounded individual. To appear especially round, include:

1. TEAM ACTIVITIES. Employers want to know you are a team player who works well with others. Indulge them by listing the many college sports teams you helped lead to victory. It would be superfluous to note that you provided this help not by playing, but by standing in the bleachers and shouting, *"We want a pitcher, not a belly it-cher!"*

Another way to illustrate your strengths as a team player is to add the word "team" onto any activity you choose. Again, make sure these activities are diverse: needlepoint **team**; coin-collecting **team**; the dream **team**.[4]

---

[4] *If you use this activity, modify the "name" section of your résumé to read: "Michael Jordan."*

2. HUMANITARIAN ACTIVITIES. Do not be so modest as to neglect mentioning that you're a Big Brother or Sister to eighty-seven malnourished Bosnian orphans, or that you fearlessly retrieved Baby Jessica from that twelve-foot well in Texas a few years back.

3. OFFBEAT ACTIVITIES. Your résumé should always include some fun-loving activities to show gullible employers you will be good for office morale. Do not include any fun-loving activities that rely too heavily upon mind-altering chemicals. Instead, select a wholesome fun-loving activity, such as puppetry. Now *that* is f-u-n, fun!

V. SKILLS: Be selective. Choose only "résumé skills" that will help get you hired.

EXAMPLES OF RÉSUMÉ SKILLS:

- making airplane and hotel reservations for others
- agreeing
- being financially independent
- being blood relative of boss
- being "fluent in" all foreign languages
- being "familiar with" all computer programs
- having "knowledge of" all else

VI. REFERENCES: Some Pre-Employed Lifers make the mistake of writing "references available on request." This statement pushes the boundaries of dishonesty. It says to an employer: "I do not have any references so I will simply put this barefaced untruth on my résumé and hope no one checks." Cheap lies will not impress your potential employer. Elaborate, sophisticated lies will.

Keeping in mind what you have learned about fraudulent résumé construction, follow along as we examine one outstanding example:

Pop Quiz

ARE YOU LIVING IN THE REAL WORLD?

1. Do you know the difference between "good" cholesterol and "bad" cholesterol?
2. Do you own a vacuum cleaner? (ten bonus points for twentieth-century models)
3. Are you *definitely* hiring movers next time?
4. Do you send "season's greetings" cards?
5. Is there a special cutlery divider tray in your silverware drawer?

DECONSTRUCTING A RÉSUMÉ

John Eric Schwartz —————————————— SEÑOR JUAN-CARLOS ENRICO SUAREZ
P.O. Box 233
42nd St. YMCA —————————— N.Y., N.Y. 10003
(212) 555-4398

Career Objective: An entry-level position allowing me to utilize my skills of making an obscene amount of money for my potential employer.

Education

*Middlesex County Junior
Vocational Tech
Community College
Correspondence School*

Harvard University: BA, PhD, MA, MC, MD, MFA, BFA, BS graduate spring 1994. Double Major: Brain Surgery/Acting as Liaison. Phi
High School Equivalency Beta Kappa. GPA: 5.0
Academic probation

0.5 **London School of Economics:** MBA, CPA, DDS, BM, MS, MSW, OT, RN, LPN. Fall, 1993. Rhodes scholar. Major: Neo-quantum geophysics litiga-
tion. Voted ''most likely to act as a liaison.''
*Newark School
of Auto Repair*

Enrolled Fall, 1983 **Maximum Ability Day Care Centre for Gifted Children**
Road paver

*Major: brake pad
replacement* *Professional Experience*

*Maximum Security
Detention Center
for Troubled Youth* **Supreme Commander of the Universe** *creation-present*
Act as liaison between staff of 250 billion human beings and lower species. Implemented use of light, initiated environment, coor-
dinated widespread phenomena including ice age, global warming, static cling, life as we know it. Oversaw evolution of man from ape; sired Winona Ryder.
  Awards and Honors: recipient of numerous national holidays; worshiped by many, many people.

POSSIBLE **Seating Czar**, Loews Coliseum of Motion Picture Arts and Sciences,
FABRICATION *fall 1992*
Culled and collated quadrillions of ticket vouchers, manually se-
vered into equivalent halves, and redistributed to members of cul-
Usher tural elite. Led and directed tardy clients into screening facility with use of battery-operated illumination implement; acted as liaison between adhesive flooring and mop. Coined
*One night in October
(quit without giving notice)* phraseology, ''Thank you for coming to Loews, sit back and relax, enjoy the show.''

Price Sticker Boy

Chief Executive Officer of Finance, Victuals Metropolis, *summer 1991*
Applied market prices to common stock utilizing advanced trigger technology. Duties included managing transference of numerous solid and liquid assets from private holdings to OTC sales. Acted as liaison between consumer and cash Registrar. Voted Fastest Chief Executive Officer of Finance of the Month.

Foodtown

NASA Aerospace Engineer, *spring 1990*
Walked on moon. Led 10 astronauts on lunar research expedition to interior of simulated interplanetary surface; evaluated gravitational force upon human vertical locomotion. Acted as liaison.

Bounced around in "moonwalk" ride with 10 friends during college carnival

Prime Minister of Public Relations, M. C. Donalds & Co., Ltd., *winter*
Represented global nutritional conglomerate with annual product distribution of billions and billions. Implemented off-site poultry sampling focus groups; acted as wardrobed liaison between deep-fried nuggets of fowl and 5 dipping sauces. Extensive public speaking.

Dressed up in Chicken McNugget costume and passed out free samples while clucking

Liaison, Liaisons R Us, Inc., *winter, spring, summer, fall*
Duties included implementing, coordinating, assessing, gathering, directing, executing, and providing support.

COMPLETE FABRICATION

Activities
Captain, Pro-Am Golf Team; Linebacker, Miami Dolphins; Olympic water ballet team; baking team; varsity sumo wrestling team. Initiated/coordinated/implemented ''Earth Day'': 1990; heroically dove into raging Atlantic Ocean to rescue 15 drowning children during Hurricane Andrew: Miami, 1992; puppetry.

Once caddied at uncle's golf club

Still goes around saying, "Hasta la vista, baby."

Skills
Fluent *Español*, et al.; familiar with Microsoft Word, Wordperfect, Excel; knowledge of DOS, Solomon, Adobe, Claris Works, XyWrite, Quark, Fortran, File Maker, Lotus 123, Lotus 456.

Familiar with "Pong"

Additional skills: too numerous to mention.

HOW TO FIND YOUR DREAM JOB

1. Fall asleep
2. Dream
3. Find job

WHAT TO DO WHEN YOU WAKE UP

The first thing you must do is network. Networking, it has been pointed out, sounds very much like *not*working. This isn't the case at all. Networking sounds much more like "wetnerking." Unfortunately, you will never get a job by "wetnerking," since that is not a word.

To network successfully, you need two things: (1) a Rolodex (2) a card. Just because you do not have a job is no excuse not to have a card. Why not pass out a baseball card? If you are not a sports fan, simply rummage through your wallet each time you meet a potential employer and repeat the following phrase:

"How embarrassed I am to be out of business cards! Do you have something I can write on?"

Soon you will be ready to go through your Rolodex and list your well-connected professional contacts. If you are like most Pre-Employed Lifers, your list will be similar to this:

1. Bubba from Thrifty Discount Beverage

BUILDING YOUR NETWORK

At first, your list of well-connected professional contacts may appear rather limited. But once you tap into *Bubba*'s professional network, you'll multiply your connections and gain access to a pipeline of VIPs. Simply construct a "professional networking tree" like this one:

Pop Quiz

ARE YOU LIVING IN THE REAL WORLD?

1. Have you shortened/lengthened your first name in the past five years?
2. Have you gone to a dinner party in the past five weeks?
3. Do you have renters' insurance?
4. Do you have a shopping list?
5. Do you save twisty-ties?

BUBBA FROM THRIFTY DISCOUNT BEVERAGE

1. Bubba's mother (FINANCE CONNECTIONS: once met someone who knows woman who vacuums floor at First National)

2. Bubba's father (PUBLISHING CONNECTIONS: had letter to editor published in *Processed Cheese Food Journal*)

3. Bubba's brother (LAW CONNECTIONS: prisoner)

4. Bubba's sister (SCIENCE CONNECTIONS: cosmetologist)

5. Bubba's brother-in-law (TRAVEL INDUSTRY CONNECTIONS: plays poker with neighbor of TWA luggage-cart driver)

6. Bubba's nephew (SOCIAL SERVICES CONNECTIONS: collects cans in park)

7. Bubba's niece (CHILDREN'S SERVICES CONNECTIONS: Girl Scout)

8. Bubba's third cousin once removed (SHOW BUSINESS CONNECTIONS: frequently sees shows.)

9. Bubba's friend (COMPUTER CONNECTIONS: knows someone who went to nursery school with Steve Jobs's prom date)

10. Bubba's friend's friend (FASHION INDUSTRY CONNECTIONS: once returned ripped shirt to Banana Republic and received apology letter stating: "Please let us know if there is any way we can help you in the future.")

HOW TO SCHMOOZE

Schmoozing sounds very much like "using," and for good reason. It entails talking politely to others just so you can turn the conversation around to your job hunt. If you are concerned that this job-hunting technique will make you feel like a manipulative, opportunistic sleaze, fear not. If you were a manipulative, opportunistic sleaze, you would be running your own business by now.

For maximum schmooze potential, utilize the strategies below:

FOUR SIMPLE SCHMOOZE MOVES

1. NAME-DROP. In the Real schmoozing World, it's all *who* you know—not who knows *you*. Let us assume you are an aspiring scriptwriter. The next time you find yourself chatting with a famous Hollywood producer, name-drop thusly:

"ARNOLD SCHWARZENEGGER, whom I have known since childhood, says I could net millions on my screenplay, especially since my sister MICHELLE PFEIFFER and my roommate JULIA ROBERTS want to star. Uncle FRANCIS FORD COPPOLA is dying to direct, but MADONNA keeps telling me to go with SPIKE LEE, my brother. Do you know anyone who'd be interested in producing?"

2. GET REACQUAINTED WITH THOSE YOU'VE ALIENATED. Many people you have mistreated in the past are now much more successful than you. Why not track them down and patch things up?:

"Hello? Is this Nathan Mellman, director of hiring for a large multinational organization? Nathan, I'm not sure you'll remember me, but I'm the one who threw your napkin holder out the window in seventh-grade metal shop. Oh, you do? Great! Listen, now that we're adults, I wanted to let you know I'm capable of committing far more grisly acts to anyone who doesn't give me what I want. Do you happen to have any job openings?"

3. ACT AS IF YOU'RE INTERESTED IN PEOPLE. Should you meet someone in a position to hire you, ask about his or her family and leisure-time activities. When you get home, enter the person's name in your Rolodex, followed by several facts you have gleaned. Phone regularly just to see how they're doing:

"Hello there, Amelia R. Buttonweezer, date of birth 9/7/45, whom I met April 12th at my parents' anniversary party. How is your 5' 11" Caucasian male husband, Kenneth, and your lovely eldest daughter, Minnie, a freshman at Slippery Rock University? Are you still an avid collector of S&H green stamps? Well, I just wanted to say hi. I certainly wasn't calling to see if you were still looking for a personal secretary."

4. DON'T STOP WHEN YOU FIND A JOB. Even after you've finally found employment, schmoozing is the best way to continue moving up in the world. Suppose you are at work and you hear some people discussing an exciting job opportunity. Walk over and ask if they'd like to have lunch:

"Hi, are you ready to order? Today's lunch special is chicken salad on toast. Would anyone like a drink to start? Do you need a couple of minutes to decide? Do you have any jobs?"

HOW TO RECOGNIZE A HELP WANTED AD

In the Real working World, there are two distinct types of Help Wanted Ads.

Help Wanted Ad 1 looks something like this:

FUTZBAUM, *Percy. Beloved son of Myra and Earl, brother of Helga. Died suddenly in his sleep. Mr. Futzbaum leaves behind a bright career as an associate implementer with the firm of Integrated Coordinators, where he will be best remembered for his selfless integrating, coordinating, and liaison acting. He will be missed by all. Funeral tomorrow morning.*

In lieu of condolences or flowers, you will want to send a résumé to Mr. Futzbaum's surviving employer immediately.

Help Wanted Ad 2 looks something like this:

ADMINISTRATIVE ASSISTANT
Dynamic, expanding company seeks hungry self-starter for entry-level position with opportunity for advancement. Ideal candidate will be an energetic go-getter with an interest in telecommunications technology. Pleasant conditions with frequent fieldwork. We offer a competitive salary.

If this seems like the job for you, you're not alone. Six thousand other people who read this ad think it is the job for them. But that should not stop you from applying. *This* should stop you from applying:

ADMINISTRATIVE ASSISTANT: **indentured servant**
DYNAMIC: **twelve hostile takeovers last year**
EXPANDING: **one employee left after layoffs**
HUNGRY: **will work for food**
SELF-STARTER: **works well with no direction; psychic ability required**
ENTRY-LEVEL: **data entry**
OPPORTUNITY FOR ADVANCEMENT: **upon quitting**

ENERGETIC: **700 w.p.m.**
GO-GETTER: **ability to go get boss's coffee, mail, Christmas gifts**
INTEREST IN TELECOMMUNICATIONS TECHNOLOGY: **interest in saying, "Good afternoon, how may I direct your call?"**
PLEASANT CONDITIONS: **above ground**
FIELDWORK: **cotton picking**
COMPETITIVE SALARY: **compared to migrant farmworker**

EMPLOYMENT AGENCIES: AN ENTRY-LEVEL SIMULATION

In addition to the ads described above, beware the telltale employment agency ad:

> WANTED: Recent grad willing to make one million dollars and travel around world. Call Mrs. Edwards between 3:30-3:36, Wednesdays.

Should you answer this ad, you will pay a visit to the *Acme Employment Agency: No Job Too Small.* You will be told that Mrs. Edwards is "unavailable,"[5] but Mr. Armstrong will see you. Mr. Armstrong will emerge three hours later. He will have a clubfoot and an eye patch. The discussion will proceed along the following lines:

MR. ARMSTRONG: Well, I see here from your résumé that you majored in international relations.

YOU: Yes, I'm particularly interested in bringing modern irrigation technology to developing Third World nations.

MR. ARMSTRONG: How fast can you type?

You will be led into a small dank room, where you will find yourself typing the following phrase 600 times: "Build a better mousetrap. Build a better mousetrap. Build a better mousetrap." When you are through with this vastly practical typing test, you will bring it back for evaluation:

MR. ARMSTRONG: You have made too many typos to qualify for the millionaire job. What are some of your other interests?

YOU: I am very interested in photography.

MR. ARMSTRONG: Photography! We have the perfect job for you! It is working in the shipping department of a soft luggage wholesale outlet.

YOU: I'm not sure that would be quite right. But I am also interested in government.

MR. ARMSTRONG: Government! We have the perfect job for you! It is a surgical supplies sales rep.

Eventually, you will realize that you've fallen prey to the old "bait and switch" technique. Nothing to be ashamed of. Now that you know better, you'll never again respond to ads that look too good to be true. You will only answer *legitimate* ads, such as the one you will spot the very next day:

> WANTED: Recent grad for glamorous career in government photography. Must be willing to bring modern irrigation technology to developing Third World nations. Call Mrs. Edwards between 3:30-3:36, Wednesdays.

[5] *nonexistent*

REDISCOVERING THE COLLEGE CAREER CENTER (AND PUB)

Even after graduation, college career placement centers can be valuable job-hunting resources. Visit the center at the nearest university if you don't live close to your own. Like you, the other Pre-Employed Lifers inside also snuck in off the street. If the center is strict about student identification, come back at night with a crowbar and a flashlight.

Once you're in, you'll discover an array of databases, bulletin boards, and notebooks brimming with job opportunities. These opportunities come in three forms:

- Jobs that have been listed since the early 1800s: *Town Crier Needed. Loud Voice, Knowledge of Current Events*
- Jobs for which you are entirely underqualified: *CEO, Global Securities and Trust. Must Have 50 Years' Experience as Bank President*
- Jobs for which you are entirely overqualified: *Freshman Wanted for Raking Once a Month*

Clearly, you should explore other options. With the money you earn from the raking job, buy a pitcher or two at the college pub. After several rounds of Thumper with the intramural badminton team, you will feel pathetic enough to go out and get a job.

ALUMNI DIS-CONNECTIONS

Many college career centers also provide phone numbers of successful alumni who are happy to speak with recent grads. Remember two things about these successful alumni. (1) Most of them are dead. (2) The rest of them are not really so successful. If they were, they would be too busy working to waste their time talking to you.

ACING THE INFORMATIONAL INTERVIEW

To increase your chances of scheduling an informational interview, make it clear that you are not looking for a job. "I am *not* looking for a job," you should say. "Instead, I am a curious Pre-Employed Lifer interested in exploring many fields and gleaning pearls of wisdom from the leaders I most admire."

Because the informational interview is *not* a real job interview, you're the one who'll be expected to ask all the questions. Here is a short list to get you started:

1. What kind of salary are you offering me?
2. When do I start?
3. Where is my company car/yacht/jet?
4. Where is my company parking space/marina/airplane hangar?
5. What is my secretary's name?
6. How many windows are in my office?
7. How large is my expense account?
8. How long is my vacation?
9. What are my stock options?
10. Get me my coffee and hold my calls, will ya?

INTERNSHIPS: ARE THEY FOR YOU?

With a dearth of job openings, many Pre-Employed Lifers opt for unpaid internships, hoping they will get hired when something becomes available. This rarely works out. In the Real World, the *student* intern will get hired when something becomes available. After all, at least he or she is licking envelopes, stamps, and boots for college credit. You, on the other hand, are doing it for nothing. What employer in their right mind would hire a chump like that?

Pop Quiz

ARE YOU LIVING IN THE REAL WORLD?

1. Have you begun reading restaurant reviews?
2. Have you developed a taste for herbal tea?
3. How many times have you moved since graduation? (a) 0 (b) one (c) lost track
4. Do you own a shoe rack?
5. Are you friends with anyone who is five or more years older than you?

YOUR DAILY JOB-HUNTING SCHEDULE

8:00 a.m.	clock radio goes off
8:00 a.m.	hit "snooze"
8:09 a.m.	clock radio goes off
8:09 a.m.	heave clock radio against wall
9:30 a.m.	stumble into kitchen for breakfast: one slice cold pizza, 5 cups coffee
9:45 a.m.	get newspaper for Help Wanteds
9:46 a.m.	read TV listings
10:00 a.m.[6]	*Regis & Kathie Lee:* Rege gets armpits, back, and fanny waxed
11:00 a.m.	rest
11:30 a.m.	check mail; return empty-handed
11:35 a.m.	drag yellow highlighter across page of Help Wanteds
11:36 a.m.	decide to "get organized": start "job file"
11:37 a.m.	search room for file folders; discover box of old letters from summer camp
11:45 a.m.	read old letters from summer camp
12:30 p.m.	write letter to old friend from summer camp
12:50 p.m.	**fleeting panic attack:** call everyone you've ever met in entire life and ask if they know of any jobs in any field anywhere in country
1:00 p.m.	*Three's Company:* Chrissy thinks Mrs. Roper has crush on her. Closed captioned for the hearing-impaired
1:30 p.m.	lunch: 2 cups Cat Chow, 6 cups coffee
1:45 p.m.	check mail; return empty-handed
1:50 p.m.	decide to "get organized": alter résumé to suit jobs in Help Wanteds
2:15 p.m.	think about going to post office to mail résumés & letter to old friend from summer camp
2:20 p.m.	go to post office to mail résumés & realize you don't have address of old friend from summer camp
2:40 p.m.	decide to "get organized": go to stationery store to buy new address book
3:40 p.m.	return from stationery store with industrial file cabinet, 16 pen refills, new address book
3:45 p.m.	begin transferring names from old address book into new address book

Pop Quiz

ARE YOU LIVING IN THE REAL WORLD?

1. Have you ever paid to park in a garage?
2. Have you ever conducted a garage sale?
3. Do you secretly enjoy rolling around on the wheels of your office chair?
4. Have you eaten free Happy Hour hors d'oeuvres for dinner in the past three weeks?
5. Does your bed have a box spring?

6 check local listings

3:55 p.m	**fleeting panic attack:** call human resources departments of random companies in yellow pages
4:00 p.m.	*Maury Povich:* grads who bludgeon human resources employees to death
4:01 p.m.	turn off TV; make list of "things to do"
4:05 p.m.	do laundry; try to balance checkbook during spin cycle; fail
5:30 p.m.	return from laundromat
5:35 p.m.	iron clothes
6:00 p.m.	fold clothes
6:30 p.m.	carefully place clothes on hangers
6:45 p.m.	store clothes in closet
7:00 p.m.	decide to "get organized": reorganize closet
8:00 p.m.	dinner: 4 glasses Jack Daniel's, 3 cubes ice
8:05 p.m.	decide freezer needs defrosting
8:06 p.m.	call mother to find out how to defrost freezer
8:07 p.m.	mother asks about job search
8:08 p.m.	inform mother of sudden emergency call on other line
8:09 p.m.	feel guilty
8:10 p.m.	check mail; return with Lillian Vernon catalog
8:11 p.m.	think about reading career guide
8:12 p.m.	think about reading Lillian Vernon catalog
8:13 p.m.	read Lillian Vernon catalog
8:14 p.m.	have another glass of dinner
9:00 p.m.	pass out
4:00 a.m.	**fleeting panic attack:** wake up in cold sweat wondering what you're doing with your life
4:01 a.m.	decide to "get organized": order special SleepEeez Snap-On Collar Comfort Pillow from Lillian Vernon catalog

Pop Quiz

ARE YOU LIVING IN THE REAL WORLD?

1. Do you own *The Joy of Cooking* and/or *The Moosewood Cookbook*?
2. Have you ever gone to someone's home for dinner and returned with a written recipe?
3. Do you have any sort of special insoles in your shoes?
4. Are your ice cube trays always full of ice?
5. Do you have a doormat?

TEMP YOUR WAY TO THE TOP!

The goal of temping is to land a permanent job by getting the person you are filling in for fired. This is easier than ever. Employers have discovered that hiring temps at low wages with no benefits is more efficient than hiring employees at low wages with no benefits. It eliminates the need to learn the names of those who work for them.

Still, do not expect to breeze into a temp job if you do not have the proper skills. The proper skills are: (a) looking good in a dress, and (b) ability to speak aloud.

How to Get Your Predecessor Fired
Let's call the person you're replacing Bernice. Bernice has been placed in intensive care after being run over by a truck. Follow these steps to steal Bernice's job before she recovers:

STEP ONE: Set the stage early for Bernice's termination with a few carefully placed comments. Try this: "I'll tell you one thing, Bernice is going to have a hard time doing all this stapling with both arms amputated."

STEP TWO: After you've got the buzz going with Bernice's coworkers, move on to her boss. Each day, inform him of a new mistake you've discovered she's made. Start small by mentioning that report she misstapled. Move on to something larger, such as the twenty thousand dollars you've discovered she embezzled from the company.

Eventually, your integrity will get you noticed by the supervisor. "Hey, you!" he will say. "What is your name?"

STEP THREE: Once you've turned the entire office against Bernice, gain favor for yourself. Flatter. Hug. Bring everyone long-stemmed roses. Soon enough, sickly old Bernice will get the ax and you will be recognized as the best man for the job. Buy yourself a new dress to celebrate.

THE FIVE-SECOND CAREER COUNSELOR

If the job search leaves you more confused than ever, you may want to hire a career counselor. Bear in mind that it is not a career counselor's job to *find* you a job. If they found you a job, then *they* would be out of a job. Therefore, all they really want to do is confuse you even more. You do not need to pay someone to do that.

CONCOCTING A COVER LETTER: THE MAD-LIB TECHNIQUE

Once you've identified some jobs to fall into, send your résumé with a cover letter explaining your interest. Do not send it to the personnel department. These people are functionally illiterate. Instead, send it to the president of the company. He or she has assistants to help with the hard words.

It would be unprofessional to send the same cover letter to every company in your preferred field. This is because you do not know what your preferred field *is*. Therefore, compose a new cover letter for any and all fields that happen to have a position open. Do not worry if these fields are of no interest to you, or even if you don't understand the first thing about the position for which you are applying. All it takes is a thoughtfully customized cover letter to show employers how much you want the job. Follow the example on the next page:

Dear **Dr. Scholl**
(president of company)

Your **MOTHER** , **the late MRS. SCHOLL**, suggested I write you
(alleged job connection) *(proper noun)*

regarding the job opening in your firm. I have always

dreamed of becoming a **Regional Unit Amalgamations Synthesizer, Orthotics Division** .
(title of available job)

My interest in **feet** dates back to my **Intro. to Podiatry**
(specific component of job) *(relevant coursework)*

at **Harvard University**, from which I recently graduated.
(Harvard University)

In addition to **playing FOOTball** I also worked part-time
(extracurricular activity)

at **Woolworths**, where I **often reordered shoe deodorizing products** .
(name of corporation) *(job skills acquired)*

There is nothing I like doing more in my free time than

regional unit amalgamations synthesizing .
(related hobby)

I hope you'll agree that I would be a perfect match for

Dr. Scholls . Enclosed you will find my résumé.
(name of company)

THE NEXT STEP: RECEIVING YOUR REJECTION LETTER

All you have to do now is sit back and wait for those rejections to pour in. See? This process is not that different from applying to colleges, is it? No longer will you take rejection letters personally, however. Instead, you'll look at them as constructive, useful tools . . . .

HOW TO MAKE THE MOST OF REJECTION LETTERS

1. place mat

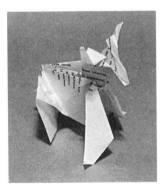
2. origami

3. heat

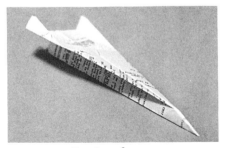
5. aircraft

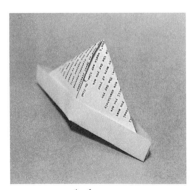
4. hat

WHAT IF I DON'T GET REJECTED?

If, for some reason, a certain company does not send a rejection letter, always call to see what the holdup is. As long as you're calling, try arranging an interview as well.

When calling to arrange an interview, never take no for an answer. To do this, hang up immediately after asking the question, "Can we arrange an interview?" Otherwise, you will engage in the following conversation:

POTENTIAL EMPLOYER: Hello, this is Dick Johnson.

YOU: Good afternoon, Mr. Johnson. I'm calling to follow up on the résumé I sent you eight and a half months ago. I was hoping we could arrange an inter—

POTENTIAL EMPLOYER: I'm either away from my desk or on another line. Press one if you'd like to leave a message on my voice mail. Press two if you'd like to leave a message on my assistant's voice mail. No one is ever going to speak to you directly. No one will ever return your messages. We know you want a job. Never call here again. If you do, I will have you arrested. This call has already been traced to your home. If you are calling from a rotary phone, please stay on the line and a switchboard operator will be with you shortly.

Do not be put off by this standard screening procedure. When the operator asks what your call is regarding, simply say it is regarding Mr. Johnson's "blood test." You'll get Dick on the phone pronto. Tell him the switchboard operator must have misunderstood. Ask him if you can arrange an interview. Hang up immediately.

HOW TO BLUFF YOUR WAY THROUGH AN INTERVIEW

If you are lucky enough to get called in for an interview, remember: The key is to prepare yourself by researching the company. Before going into your interview, always pull the re-

ceptionist aside and say, "So what does this company do again?"

DRESS FOR STRESS

The goal here is to distinguish yourself from the several hundred Brooks brothers and sisters waiting in the reception area to interview for *your* job. Therefore, never wear the ridiculous business suit you got as a graduation gift. Wear a sweatsuit. This type of suit more effectively absorbs the pool of perspiration you will produce while waiting in the reception area.

Seconds before the actual interview, bring your garment bag into the bathroom and change into the ridiculous business suit you got as a graduation gift. Also, change into the Depends diapers you brought in case you wet yourself during a particularly tough question.[7]

HOW TO LOOK PROFESSIONAL. Looking professional can win you a second interview. However, it will be difficult to look professional on the second interview because you will be wearing the same ridiculous suit you wore on the first interview—only now it will be damper. Still, there is no need to go out and shoplift another career costume. Instead, learn to accessorize. Wear a different shirt with the same pants; tie an attractive scarf or ascot around your neck; wear gloves.

CAREER-SPECIFIC ACCESSORIZING. Never wear a backwards baseball cap to an interview unless applying for the job of umpire. Wear a nose ring strictly when interviewing to be an anthropologist. As for tartan-plaid kilts, they are considered appropriate for aspiring bagpipers, who should always be interviewed in oxygen-free soundproof booths. No matter what job you're interviewing for, you'll *really* wow your interviewers by showing up with the company tote bag flung casually over your shoulder.

What about proper attire for other typical jobs? Herewith, an illustrated compendium:

[7] *"How are you?"*

HOW TO DRESS
GROWING FIELDS OF

Pop Quiz

ARE YOU LIVING IN THE REAL WORLD?

1. Have you developed a newfound fondness for documentaries?
2. Have you ever washed your shower curtain?
3. Is your driver's license issued from the state in which you now drive?
4. Are you registered to vote in the state in which you now reside?
5. Do you plan for New Year's Eve several months in advance?

sandwich board sign

blanket wrapped around shoulders

tin can

PLEASE HELP ME! I AM A RECENT COLLEGE GRAD

starving dog

Bachelor of Arts diploma

FIDO

BEGGAR.

bandanna around mouth

gun

valise

BANK ROBBER.

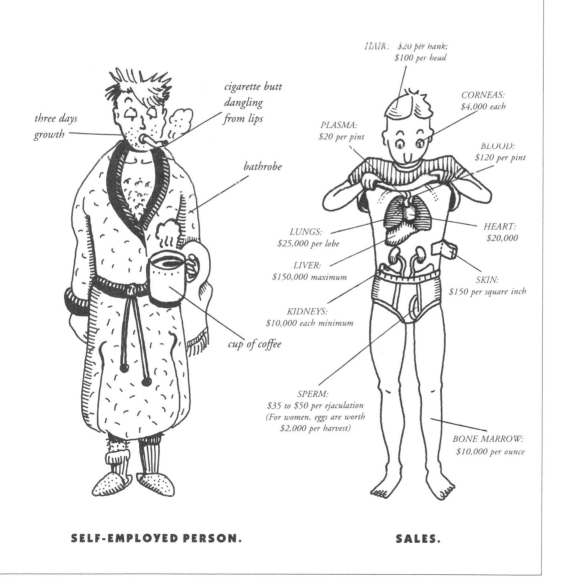

three days
growth

cigarette butt
dangling
from lips

bathrobe

cup of coffee

SELF-EMPLOYED PERSON.

HAIR: $20 per hank;
$100 per head

CORNEAS:
$4,000 each

PLASMA:
$20 per pint

BLOOD:
$120 per pint

LUNGS:
$25,000 per lobe

HEART:
$20,000

LIVER:
$150,000 maximum

SKIN:
$150 per square inch

KIDNEYS:
$10,000 each minimum

SPERM:
$35 to $50 per ejaculation
(For women, eggs are worth
$2,000 per harvest)

BONE MARROW:
$10,000 per ounce

SALES.

TEN TRICK INTERVIEW QUESTIONS: THINK BEFORE YOU ANSWER

1. How did you choose your college?

WHAT YOU THINK: It was the only one I got into.

WHAT YOU ANSWER: It was the best of all ten that recruited me for a full academic scholarship.

2. Tell me something you learned in school that could be used on the job.

WHAT YOU THINK: That Aristotle emphasized the observation of nature and stressed that virtue is a mean between extremes.

WHAT YOU ANSWER: How to budget my time to meet deadlines.

3. What have you been doing since graduation?

WHAT YOU THINK: Groveling before people like you for a job.

WHAT YOU ANSWER: Holding out for the perfect job, and, frankly, I believe I've found it.

4. Are you willing to take a drug test before being hired?

WHAT YOU THINK: Oh my God.

WHAT YOU ANSWER: As a thoroughly prepared, highly motivated job candidate, I have already made it my duty to undergo a drug test, and I am pleased to report the results are entirely negative.

5. Where do you want to be five years from now?

WHAT YOU THINK: In Barbados.

WHAT YOU ANSWER: In management.

6. What's your biggest flaw?

WHAT YOU THINK: What are you, my mother?

WHAT YOU ANSWER: I'm a perfectionist.

7. How long do you plan to stay with our company?

WHAT YOU THINK: Until the interview is done.

WHAT YOU ANSWER: For the rest of my life.

8. Why did you leave your last job?

WHAT YOU THINK: Job?

WHAT YOU ANSWER: Creative differences.

9. Do you have any questions for me?

WHAT YOU THINK: What's the deal with that thing in your teeth?

WHAT YOU ANSWER: What has been the growth cycle of the company over the last five years?

10. Tell me, hotstuff, what are you wearing underneath that sexy suit?

WHAT YOU THINK: Diapers.

WHAT YOU ANSWER: Um . . . What has been the growth cycle of the company over the last five years?

Pop Quiz

ARE YOU LIVING IN THE REAL WORLD?

1. Is there an extra room in your apartment that is not being used to absolute maximum capacity?

2. Do you use the plastic divider bar to separate your groceries at the checkout line?

3. Have you ever given the following advice?: "Drive carefully."

4. Have you ever asked the following question: "Seen any good movies lately?"

5. Have you ever trimmed your nose hair?

BODY LANGUAGE

Just as important as what you say during an interview is what your body is saying about you, so be sure to conceal any tattoos that say: "Work sucks, let's party." Below, a guide to your body's other nonverbal signals:

EYES: Rolling your eyes upward is a good way to show that you think a question is particularly dumb. Rolling them completely behind your head to expose the white sockets, however, sends a negative message that you are a health insurance risk. Since it is important to maintain eye contact, never cover your eyes with your hands when answering a question, except if you are in tears. Flip your eyelids inside out to demonstrate versatility. Finally, crossing your eyes playfully every so often shows your interviewer that you'll maintain a nutty sense of humor even in a high-pressure situation.

HANDS: Clasping your hands together before the interview shows that you are engaged in deep prayer. To greet your interviewer, use the two-handed handshake if you wish to demonstrate that you are an insincere, "emotional" type. Clapping of the hands shows your interviewer that you are pleased. Lurching over the desk with clenched hands suggests that you are dissatisfied. Using sign language shows that you are deaf.

FEET: Tapping your feet sends out a signal that you have rhythm, though a slow tap in conjunction with the upward eye roll may be interpreted as a sign of impatience. Playing "footsie" with your interviewer, especially in combination with eyelash-batting, suggests you are someone who will "go all the way" for the right job.

NOSE: Crinkling your nose, sniffing, and saying, "What stinks in here?" suggests a highly developed sense of smell. Twitching your nose rapidly from side to side suggests you are Elizabeth Montgomery.

HAIR: Pulling out of the hair demonstrates frustration, particularly if the hair is attached to the interviewer.

BUTTOCKS: Breaking wind during an interview says: "I have poor eating habits, do not hire me."

NON-BODY LANGUAGE: WORDS

Saying words is another important part of the interview process. However, some modification of your current vocabulary may be in order. The following chart will help you become articulate in the Real-Worldly sense of the word.

UNREAL-WORLDLY LANGUAGE	REAL-WORLDLY LANGUAGE
"So I go, so she goes, so I go, so she goes . . ."	"So I said, so she said, so I said, so she said . . ."
"Awesome!"	"Satisfactory!"
"Totally!"	"Entirely so!"
"Not."	"I am jesting of course."
"Like, ya know? I always, like wanted to be, like a secretary?"	"I have always wanted to be a secretary."
"Bogus"	"Untrue"
"No way!"	"Is that so?"
"Duh!"	"I believe that point is self-evident."
"That sucks."	"That is unfortunate."
"Later, dude/babe."	"Goodbye, sir/madam."

THE GRAND FINALE: SCENES FROM AN INTERVIEW

It is often useful to think of an interview as a play.[8] To help you vary your acting technique accordingly, we now present two classic dramatic interpretations of *The Entry-Level Interview*. Rehearse each script at home with roommates, and remember: Whatever you do, just don't be yourself.

THE LOW-PRESSURE INTERVIEW

SCENE: A large, sunny office. The INTERVIEWER, wearing an earthtone shawl, sits behind a warm, cherrywood desk. As a recording of the RAIN FOREST plays softly in the background, she eats RICE CAKES. A PRE-EMPLOYED LIFER sits opposite her. The INTERVIEWER's motivation is to dispense with corporate dogma and get to know the PRE-EMPLOYED LIFER on a more personal level. The PRE-EMPLOYED LIFER's motivation is to demonstrate the proper karma.

　　INTERVIEWER studies résumé, looks up, and . . . Action!

INTERVIEWER (smiling): If you're comfortable with this, I thought a good way to get to know each other might be if you told me a little something about yourself, if you don't mind.
PRE-EMPLOYED LIFER: Well, I'm a loving, caring person who, like you, places great importance upon personal human interaction.

INT: I feel very close to you already. Tell me, have you ever thought about why you'd like to work for this particular company?
PEL (confidently): Yes.
INT: Great. Listen, I was admiring your belt. Where did you ever find it?
PEL (maintaining eye contact): At Belts 'N' Things.
INT: They just opened down the street, didn't they?
PEL (smiling sagely): I was hoping you'd ask that question. Actually, they opened one and a half months ago, with a wide selection of all the latest styles. (*pause for effect*) No animals were harmed in the production of this belt.

PHONE *rings.*

INT: Oh hi, dumpling, how's your day going? Can you pick up some soy milk on the way home? Listen, I'm sort of in the middle of a discussion-view right now. Call-ya-later-love-ya-lots!
INT (hangs up, assumes lotus position): Where were we? Oh yes. Now, if you don't mind me asking, I was wondering: Who would you say your role model is?
PEL (without missing a beat): Who's yours?
INT: Shirley MacLaine.
PEL: Mine, too.
INT: When can you start?

(*They embrace. Fade to black*)

---

[8] *usually a tragedy*

THE HIGH-PRESSURE INTERVIEW

SCENE: A cramped, darkened office. The INTERVIEWER, wearing a polyester suit with stains under the armpits, sits behind an enormous steel desk. A powerful spotlight shines directly into the eyes of the PRE-EMPLOYED LIFER opposite him. The INTERVIEWER's motivation is to make the PRE-EMPLOYED LIFER cry. The PRE-EMPLOYED LIFER's motivation is to demonstrate nerves of steel.

INTERVIEWER studies résumé, looks up, and . . . ACTION!

INTERVIEWER (sneering): What in God's name do you have to say for yourself?
PRE-EMPLOYED LIFER (maintaining eye contact): Well, I'm a hardnosed son of a bitch, who, like you, is driven by the bottom line and the quest to stay lean and mean in the marketplace.
INT: Bullshit! You're nothing but a no-good lying dropout who's never worked an honest day in your life. What in the hell gives you the right to think you'd like to work for this particular company?
PEL (putting face directly into INTERVIEWER's): Listen, you ball-buster, I've researched this company up and down. (*pause for effect*) I want this job so bad, I taste blood.
INT (nodding approvingly, scribbling notes): Not bad. What were our third-quarter gross revenues in the Atlanta division?
PEL (arrogantly): Don't toy with me.

PHONE *rings.*

INT: Oh, yeah? Well you can tell that piss-poor mama's boy to go fuck himself. Whaddaya mean he wants his money? I'm not paying that two-timing, low-down scumbag a goddamn nickel!

INT (slams down phone, removes assault rifle from wall display): Where were we? Oh yeah—Now, who's your role mod—I mean, *Look, you sniveling namby-pamby patsy-watsy college clown, who in the name of Christ almighty can you possibly have the gall to call your role model?*
PEL (without missing a beat): Who's yours?

INT (points rifle at PRE-EMPLOYED LIFER): Who wants to know?
PEL (turning tables): Look, do you want this job or not? (shouting) WHO. IS. YOUR. ROLE MODEL!
INT: General Douglas MacArthur, sir!
PEL: Mine, too.
INT (impressed; fires shot at ceiling): Not bad, you drooling, good-for-nothing sniveling slob. You make me SICK! When can you drag your sorry ass in here to start?

(*They salute. Fade out*)

KILLER FOLLOW-UP LETTERS

After your interview, write a killer follow-up letter to persuade interviewers you would kill for this job. Even if the interview was a failure, most employers will be happy to reconsider your application. Follow the example below:

Mr. Dick Johnson

Quik-Stop Shopping Center parking lot

Pawtucket, Rhode Island 02860

Dear Mr. Johnson:

Many thanks for taking time out for our meeting yesterday. I hope you found the interview to be as mutually beneficial as did I.

If you value your life, you will give me the job. If not, I will make you sorry you ever laid eyes upon me. I am going to destroy you. I know the way your daughter walks to school. I will stop at nothing in my bloodthirsty quest to annihilate you and anything you've ever loved in your wretched, fragile life. Found your missing poodle yet? I wasn't kidding in the interview when I said my hobby was taxidermy. I'm waiting for you, Dickey boy. When you least expect it, expect it.

Again, my sincere gratitude for your time. Hope to hear from you soon.

Very truly yours,

Dave Eastman-Kodak Scavullo

SECTION

III

Entry-Level Office Life

LIFE AT

Congratulations, Lifer, you've landed a job! The first thing you'll want to do before quitting is take a well-deserved *paid vacation*. These two words uttered in the same breath may sound too good to be true, but that is only because they are usually preceded by these two words: "one week." For the Working Lifer accustomed to spring break, summer vacation, and school holidays ranging from four weeks to four years, a mere five-day hiatus may seem insufficient. But *do not lose sight of your long-term career goal.*

WHAT IS MY LONG-TERM CAREER GOAL?

Your long-term career goal is to spend the least amount of time possible on the job. Ambitious? Certainly. Impossible? Dare to *dream*, Lifer! Once you've mastered the Entry-Level science of "vacation augmentation," that nagging nine-to-five commitment will never again interrupt important leisure time. Just remember this simple vacation equation:

$$1 \text{ week} = 1 \text{ year}$$

How can this be? Let us backtrack for a moment to basic college algebra—a chilling notion, but one that carries far greater rewards in the Real World. See for yourself as we prove our equation with the following algebraic symbols:

SD = Sick Day. (*number of days you are permitted to become physically ill + number of days you call work, fake-cough, and return to bed*)

PD = Personal Day. (*number of days required for job-related anxiety disorders. No faking required*)

BD = Business Day. (*number of days boss believes you are engaged in "business travel" + number of days boss believes you are "working at home"*)

DIF = Death in Family. (*number of relatives you kill off annually, real or imagined*)

HD = Half-day. (*number of days you are permitted to go home early + number of days boss is out of town*)

THE BOTTOM

CH = Company Holiday. (*number of standard holidays + all Jewish holidays[1] + Ramadan + Kwanza*)

JD = Jury Duty. (*number of days to deliberate over lengthy court case you are not at liberty to discuss with supervisors. Especially since it is being tried by Judge Joseph Wapner.*)

ML = Maternity Leave (*number of days necessary to simulate birth and care of make-believe baby*)[2]

HOW TO ACHIEVE YOUR LONG-TERM CAREER GOAL

Maximizing time away from the office is as simple as totaling the figures above. First, remove a calendar and calculator from the nearest non-corner office. With your new calendar, choose only vacation dates that can be combined with company holidays, thereby stockpiling your own allotment. Next, use your new calculator to determine the *real* number of paid vacation days to which you are entitled. Here is a model based on our algebra refresher:

$$1(SD + 10) + 7PD + 20BD + 2DIF + (4HD + 30) + (10CH + 187 + \text{One Lunar Cycle} + 7) + 20JD + 40ML = 365 \text{ Days}$$

Hence we have proven our original equation: *1 week = 1 year*[3] Bon Voyage!

SECOND THINGS SECOND: REAPING YOUR BENEFITS

In addition to a one-year vacation, you are entitled to many other benefits, including un-

limited memo pads, highlighters, and other free household supplies from the office stockroom. There's also a no-cost, long-distance personal phone calling program; subsidized private mailing service; even individual-sized packets of Sweet'n Low. And if you're lucky enough to land a job with a company that hasn't yet filed for bankruptcy, your benefits package may also include valuable perks like:

A PAYCHECK. Few events are more emotionally charged than receiving that first check, particularly when you discover your after-tax salary. Rather than face the alarming difference between "gross"[4] and "net" pay, opt for a compensation plan known as "direct deposit." With this method, your employer transfers your pittance directly into the bank. Combined with the "direct withdrawal" system you're already using, it's the obvious choice for consistent money management.

A RETIREMENT PLAN. It's never too soon to start saving for tomorrow, especially when it is impossible to do so for today. That is why it makes sound financial sense for your company to seize any remaining money from your post-tax paycheck and invest it in an unfortunately named fund[5] which you may access as soon as you find yourself stained with age spots and playing bingo at a condominium complex in Miami Beach. Though your take-home pay may no longer cover the rent on your current home, you'll never lie awake on your park bench fretting over who'll care for you in old age.

HEALTH INSURANCE. Once you've spent six weeks filling out forms and not comprehending any of the brochures blanketing your desk, three things will be clear:

1. You now require the services of one of the optometrists described in the brochures.
2. These optometrists are located in Nebraska.

[1] *It is a federal offense for employers to inquire about religious faith.*
[2] *Male employees add ten days.*
[3] *Individual vacation time may vary. For unpaid holidays, see your travel agent and employee handbook regulations concerning "Federal Family Leave Act."*
[4] *nausea-provoking*
[5] *"Ira"*

3. Optometry is not covered by your plan.

After discussing your new HMO with the employee rep forced to explain it to you several times a week, you will learn to limit your medical emergencies strictly to those with reasonably priced deductibles.[6] But remember, the true advantage of health insurance is its sense of security. Even if you never use it, you'll always have an excuse to leave work early for "a doctor's appointment."

TOURING THE COMPOUND

By familiarizing yourself early with the lay of the land, you can choose a route to your desk that bypasses unsavory colleagues. Also, you'll observe the subtleties of office planning. Note that the farther you are placed from the middle, the more important you are. The higher the floor you're on, the more power you have. Study the plan below to become better acquainted with your new working environment.

YOUR NEW HOME

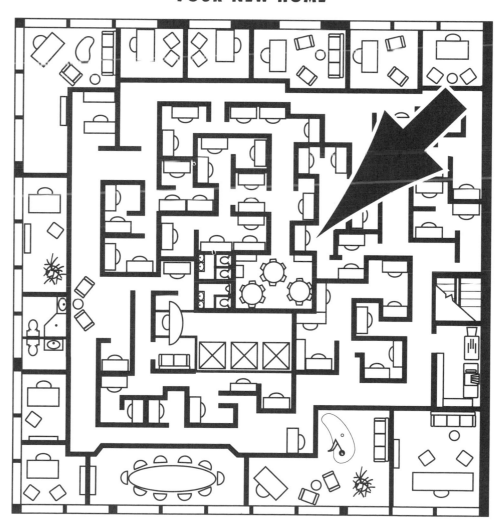

Into the Cube

Now that you're a Working Lifer, management will want you to feel right at home. And you will, since, like your new apartment, your reassuringly cramped cube has no privacy, a view of a wall, and minimal storage space. All the comforts of home—without any distracting contact with the outside world!

Office cubes are designed to keep you with the company forever. That is because you will rarely find your way out. Planned by the same architects responsible for the panic-provoking "maze of mirrors" at child-infested theme parks, the "maze of cubicles" houses a horror show in each chamber. On your right, a fellow inmate discusses his peptic ulcer on speaker phone. From your left comes something that feels like constant, deliberate kicking of the wall divider. Beware! If any other inhabitant of the maze senses you are engaged in worker productivity, it will startle you by popping its unsightly head over the partition like a nightmarish jack-in-the-box.

But that is only part of the fun. If you are with a truly progressive company, your cube walls may even be made of felt-covered cork, allowing easy air-hole puncturing with the colorful thumbtacks to which you've grown so strangely attached. Or perhaps you've landed one of those dream cubes complete with *faux*-simulated wood veneer, breathing slats, and other features traditionally found only in door-based environments. Why, as cube design continues to evolve, one can even envision the day they'll be equipped with padded rubber walls better suited to the activity that goes on inside.

For now, though, a cube is a cube is a cube. It is not a "personal work station," "cubby," or "cube-y," and it is especially not an "office," though patronizing superiors may irritatingly refer to it as such. Still, it is possible to turn your cube into so much more than a generic repository of unread mail, uneaten tunafish sandwiches, and unscrupulously obtained file cabinets you have labeled as your own and bolted down to the floor. With a healthy lack of creativity, you can transform it into a true "Cube of Distinction." How? Simply by borrowing from the elements of the cubist movement we were supposed to have read about in Intro to Art History. Consult the guide at right:

Once you've created a Cube of Distinction, you'll see that working inside isn't so bad after all, especially since it will just be a temporary stay. As long as you continue to do outstanding work, one day in the very near future, your boss is going to stride cheerfully into your cube from his five-bedroom duplex corner office with the EXECUTIVE-SIZE *faux*-simulated wood veneer desk and the lumbar-supporting crushed velour massaging desk chair and the

HELPFUL REAL WORLD TIP!

What If My Cube Does Not Have Divider Walls?

If you work in a family-style cube that has many desks in one room, you can still personalize your space. Begin with barbed-wire borders. Accessorize with such as those large, leafy plants covered with thorns, and finish things off with a juggling unicyclist mime to ensure that no one will ever invade your space.

Old-World Cubism:	Real-World Cubism:
1. Picasso	Picasso wall calendar
2. Small, disfigured bodies captured in large, blank space	large, disfigured employees captured in small, blank space
3. *Guernica*	*Doonesbury*
4. Found objects	Scotch tape dispenser, *"I'm Allergic to Morning"* mug
5. Handwritten statements addressing societal ills	Xeroxed statements addressing corporate ills: "You want It *When?!*"
6. Witty antiestablishment symbolism	Wacky wind-up penis toy or Mr. Potato Head
7. Carefully placed newspaper headlines	Carelessly stacked newspaper piles
8. Disturbing images	Family photos

leather-bound books in the fancy cherrywood shelves you've been coveting that come with cabinets that lock and those "daylight" light bulbs he doesn't even need since he's surrounded by cathedral windows overlooking the park so that not only can he grow that coconut palm tree in there while your sickly little Chia Pet withers under the fluorescent lights, but he also doesn't have to speed-dial the weather service every five minutes to find out if it's snowing or sunny or light or dark outside since *he's* not the one sitting in a sensory deprivation tank all day and *he's* not the one constantly smashing his head under his desk trying to plug his pencil sharpener into that one carefully concealed outlet that is definitely going to electrocute you if you try to fit one more plug into it, not that he would notice anyway since he's sitting comfortably at that enormous glass table he's got right in the *middle* of his receiving area in case he decides to throw a little dinner party in there for two or three hundred of his closest colleagues with the DOOR *SHUT*, while you're forced to whisper every word of *your* pressing personal phone conversations for fear of fielding embarrassing questions later from your cubemates, who have a habit of quieting down only when you're absorbed in some incredibly intimate discussion they wouldn't want to miss out on—and he's going to look you right in the eye, and he's going to shake your hand, and he's going to say . . .

"So, how do you like working in one of these nifty little offices?"

Don't blow it, Lifer. Respond with honesty and candor, and you will never have to work another day in the cube[7] again.

[7] *or the company*

MEET YOUR CUBEMATES

	HOW TO IDENTIFY:	COMMONLY FOUND:	HOW THEY GOT WHERE THEY ARE TODAY:
THE WORKAHOLIC	first in, last out	at work	no friends
THE OVERWHELMED SECRETARY	phone receiver cradled to ear while typing, faxing, computing, accounting, photocopying, mailing, filing, dialing, Advil dispensing	running company	four years at Princeton, three years at Yale, two years at Stanford
THE UNDERWHELMED MIDDLE MANAGER	Important title, impressive salary, unknown function	drawing strange organizational flow charts	delegated work to others
THE KOOKY MADCAP	performs zany *Monty Python* impressions; wears flamboyant "go to hell" wardrobe	on "creative side"	hired by Underwhelmed Middle Manager
THE GET-AHEAD CLUB	MALE MEMBERS: overdressed FEMALE MEMBERS: barely dressed	marketing, media, finance	backstabbing, throatcutting, kneeling
THE ZOMBIE	nearly lifelike	accounts receivable	only applicant for job
THE GOSSIP-MONGER	whispers	in your cube[8]	blackmail
THE PEOPLE PERSON	MALE: has mini-basketball hoop on trash can / organizes office Wally-ball league / gives you inane nickname FEMALE: sells Girl Scout cookies for daughter / asks inappropriate personal questions / compliments your ugliest shoes	human resources; company bulletin board	is a "morning person"
THE RISING STAR	recently released from cube and granted window office	in job you wanted	right place, right time
THE CRASHING METEORITE	recently removed from window office and sentenced to cube	out of the loop	demoted
THE COMPANY MAN/WOMAN	displays chromium-plated platter received for thirtieth job anniversary	in mailroom	worked way up from mailroom
THE COMPUTER WIZ	answers to name you are shrieking	retrieving data	AV club connections
THE RABBLE-ROUSER	carries army surplus backpack instead of "square" briefcase	hanging Oxfam propaganda on bulletin board; ranting about "chemicals in the workplace"	sold out
THE SCREAMING BABY	three years old, viral, quarantined from day care	within gunshot	broken condom

[8] *when you are not*

CORPORATE DEMEANOR:	BOTHERSOME WORK HABITS:	HELPFUL CAREER ADVICE:	DIRTY LITTLE SECRET:
guilt-provoking	maintains immaculate desk	"No one is indispensable."	dials 900 numbers from boss's phone after hours
hostility with a smile	reckless use of Post-it notes	"Look,I'mgonnahavetoputyouon holdandgetbacktoyoulaterwith thatbecauseasyoucanseeI'm totallyswampedsothere'snoway Icandoitbeforefivelonlyhavetwo handsandwhoareyouholdingfor?"	fantasizes about bedding UPS man in his truck
unfazed	rarely present	"You should get one of these posture-correcting stools."	sniffs Glu-Stik
intolerable	hums theme from *A Chorus Line*	"Red is definitely your color."	on antidepressants
nicey-nice	emit asphyxiating perfume/cologne fumes	"We think you'd be much happier somewhere else."	murdered freshman in hazing ritual
anesthetized	heavy sighing	" . "	nipple ring
inquisitive	compulsive door-closing	"You didn't hear it from me, but . . ."	has seen Zombie's nipple ring
relentlessly optimistic	distributes memos re-garding walkathon sponsorship, office recycling campaign, employee birthday party	"Go for it!"	once took eleven items to ten-item checkout lane
intimidating	talented, intelligent, likable	"If you believe in yourself, you can do anything."	bulimic
paranoid-possessive-defensive	won't resign	"They don't realize it now, but if they get rid of me, this place is going to fall apart."	has already hired lawyer
Golden Retrieverish	violent coughing fits	"You young people have got to be willing to pay your dues before you can ever expect to get a platter like this."	spends lunch hour interviewing for other jobs
idiot savant	obsessive-compulsive neck-cracking	"Don't write anything personal on your floppy."	picks nose and eats it
malodorous	forces you to look at Woodstock wallet photos	"Power to the motherfuckin' people."	drives BMW
contagious	spitting up	"Mommy gonna fire you."	still nursing

THE FOUR (Basically Optional) RULES OF THE WORKPLACE

**The Fifth Amendment:
Hold It In**

It is best not to urinate or defecate at the workplace. The only greater shame than moving one's bowels when one's boss walks into the lavatory is walking into the lavatory when one's boss is mid-movement. It is even more disconcerting for the male Lifer who finds himself discussing corporate infrastructure with a colleague who is relieving himself like a racehorse in the next receptacle. Conduct all waste removal off-premises. Reserve the bathroom for walking in on associates when they are doing far more embarrassing things in front of the mirror.

1 **Have a Positive Attitude.** This skill comes naturally at first because you are so grateful just to have a job, never mind one where you do not have to say, "Would you like fries with that?"[9] Besides, you feel approximately eight years old in your new office atmosphere, and everyone knows eight-year-olds just want to please. Heavy lifting? No problem! You'd *appreciate* the opportunity to change the water cooler bottle each week. Cube moved outdoors? Can do! A little lightning storm never hurt anyone.

You may eventually find it more difficult to maintain your upbeat attitude, particularly if you are not on Ecstasy. But remember, there is always something to be positive about when "attitude" is one of the categories you will be judged on in your performance review.

2 **Time Is of the Essence.** In the fast-paced Real working World, if something isn't worth doing quickly, it isn't worth doing at all. How fortunate, then, that nothing is worth doing quickly. Things especially not worth doing quickly include but are not limited to:

[9] *except during your boss's lunch hour.*

- projects you are told to do "ASAP"
- memos marked "urgent"
- letters marked "time sensitive"

This is because:

- "ASAP" is entirely subjective.
- "Urgent" memos usually deal with thermostat control.
- You may already have been chosen as one of twelve lucky winners in the Publishers Clearinghouse Sweepstakes.

3 **Be Nice to the "Little People."** Once you have been nice to yourself, it is always a good idea to be nice to the security guard and other unionized informants who are making more money than the president of the company. This is because they have accumulated so many fascinating facts about the employees who are running the company. For a cheap bottle of booze, they'll share the incriminating details you'll need to convince your boss you deserve that promotion.

4 **Never Mix Business with Pleasure.** This is by far the easiest rule to master as no effort is required.

WORKIN' NINE TO FIVE

Many Working Lifers fear that a nine-to-five schedule will be monotonous. But in the Real World, no one works nine to five anymore. Thanks to workplace advancements like "flex time," you get to stay at work after five and come in before nine; you work on Saturdays; Sundays; company holidays. And with "job-sharing," you get to do everyone else's job in addition to your own. There is certainly more to your new schedule than the eight hours you get paid for. In fact, working nine to five is the exact opposite of what most people think . . .

WORKIN' FIVE TO NINE

Adjusting to your new workaday routine will be a snap if you are the type of person who uses the word "workaday." Let us now examine an average day:

5 a.m. Commuting

On mornings you do not wake up at your desk, commuting can be one of the most rewarding parts of the campus-free lifestyle. Especially the commute home. There are several options:

1. Public Transportation: Although crowded, this is the most cost-effective method because it is free if you are good at it. It is not recommended for those who don't enjoy being felt up by formerly institutionalized passengers conducting lively debates with space aliens. Still, standing next to these individuals can provide an effective deterrent against the coworker you are pretending not to notice.

2. Car: Because your car can harm the environment, use it only when it hasn't been stolen, towed, or repossessed. To help save time, never listen to the morning traffic report, which will only land you in the vicinity of those overturned tractor trailers you've been hearing about all these years. If you are in a rush, what you need is a radar detector.

3. Bicycle: This is the most dangerous mode of commuting. As with Rollerblading, jogging, or walking, you risk arriving at work with body odor, broken limbs, or, worse, helmet-hair. To lessen your chances of being intentionally run over, memorize the following "handy hand signals":

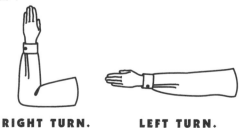

RIGHT TURN.   **LEFT TURN.**

9:00 a.m. Office Chat

Office chat requires the exchange of trivial information with your colleagues. To avoid blowing your professional cover, never share anything personal, such as a viewpoint, or a controlled substance. Don't worry that you might not be superficial or shallow enough to chat. *You* are a college graduate.

Because many offices still cannot afford liquor licenses, chat often takes place at the coffee machine or water cooler. These beverage dispensers are riveting topics of conversation themselves, to say nothing of accompanying accessories such as powdered nondairy creamer and paper cups. Other fascinating "chategories" to explore include:

work/weather/child/pet/television/sports/bad movie/weekend/lunch/weight/clothes/sale/exercise/health problem/fellow colleague

For best results, pick examples of each chategory based on chat-ee's identity. Then, simply plug these examples into the handy . . .

OFFICE CHAT PROCESSOR

"Hello there, MARY/BOB! How is the DATA ENTRY/SUPERVISING/HOLE-PUNCHING going? It is certainly a SUNNY/CLOUDY/HAZY day out there! Has little Damien WALKED/TALKED/BEEN PAROLED yet? Recently, my CAT/DOG/FISH did a cute trick. Hey, did you happen to catch SEINFELD/MURPHY

YOU CUT ME OFF, ASSHOLE.

I AM GOING TO SHOOT YOU.

Pop Quiz

ARE YOU LIVING IN THE REAL WORLD?

1. Have you ever shopped at a retail furniture store? (ten bonus points for going without parents)
2. Are you less prone to reaching heightened states of consciousness upon listening to a favorite song?
3. Are you more prone to reaching heightened states of paranoia upon inhaling a controlled substance?
4. How many weddings have you attended in the past year? (a) one (b) two (c) one too many
5. Do you use Bounce?

BROWN/FRUGAL GOURMET this week? How 'bout that BASKETBALL/BASEBALL/ AMERICAN GLADIATORS team? I think I will see the new JEAN-CLAUDE VAN DAMME/PIA ZADORA/CHEERLEADER SLUTS BEHIND BARS movie this FRIDAY/SATURDAY/SUNDAY night. Today I plan to eat CARROT STICKS/ RAISINS/SLIM-FAST for lunch as I need to lose weight so I will fit into that BATHING SUIT/BUSINESS SUIT/LEISURE SUIT that is 10/20/50% off at a nearby store. Perhaps I should increase my THIGHMASTER/AQUA-AEROBICS/ STEROID-INJECTION routine though it might aggravate my nagging GOUT/ RICKETS/SCHIZOPHRENIA. By the way, what do you think of that CUTE GUY/ HOT LITTLE NUMBER/DIRTY LYING SCHEMING HYPOCRITE over in accounting? I will see you later, MARY/BOB!"

9:01 a.m. **Do Your Job** (*refer to p. 79*)

5:00 p.m. **Lunch**

Once you become efficient, you may want to use lunch period as a time to eat. This is not recommended, as it cuts into shopping, dry cleaning, and job-sharing time. If you *must* eat, simply "brown-bag it." But remember, the days of the three-martini lunch are over—all you really need is one beer in that brown bag to successfully incapacitate yourself for the rest of the day.

Proper nutrition is not to be found in corporate cafeterias. These places are staffed by the same nonhygienic employees who spat on the mystery meat before serving it to you at your *college* cafeteria. Now that they are in the Real working World, they are spitting on the *viande mystérieuse*.

What about going out to a restaurant for lunch? There are only three justifications until you start making more money:

(1) You are eating with a friend who does not merit having dinner with.

(2) You are sipping an aperitif while waiting for hors d'oeuvres, soup, salad, entrées, dessert, cappuccino, and post-aperitif with anyone on an expense account.

(3) You are eating for a substantial discount because you moonlight as a short-order chef there three nights a week.

5:05 p.m. **Back to Work**

9:00 p.m. **Repeat "5:00 a.m." in opposite direction.**

DUES-PAYING FOR THE SHORT-TERM INVESTOR

Just because you were hired for your talent and potential does not mean these quirks will be permitted in the Real working World. The Entry-Level tradition of "paying your dues" will keep you in line. This ingenious little business theory assumes that the most promising young workers will remain loyal only if provided with demeaning, low-paid labor that has nothing to do with their written job descriptions. Why? Because that is what everyone else had to do.

If you think you might enjoy being promoted before you have grandchildren, however, many bosses are open to a literal interpretation of "dues-paying." Pay them off in monthly installments, and soon you'll get the experience you need to launch a competing business, sell it to Sony, and open that bar-café you've always dreamed of.

ARE YOU LIVING IN THE REAL WORLD?

1. Do you have a sewing kit?
2. Would you ever think of riding your bike without a helmet?
3. Is there a box of baking soda anywhere in your home?
4. Do you read two or more magazines each month that are not *J. Crew* and *Victoria's Secret*?
5. Do you own a magazine rack?

CLIMBING THE CORPORATE STAIRMASTER

With competition being what it is,[10] you might assume more experienced colleagues will block your rise up the corporate ladder. This is no longer the case, because not only have more experienced colleagues been replaced by machines, but so has the corporate ladder. With today's stationary "Corporate StairMaster," you'll get the most vigorous workplace workout possible—and never again wonder if it's getting you anywhere. All pain, no gain. Here's the latest design:

PROFESSIONAL SKILLS: A HOW-TO GUIDE

Perhaps you were the editor of your college newspaper. Perhaps you were the valedictorian of your graduating class. Perhaps you are a pathological liar. The fact is, only the last of these attributes has provided you with the professional skills you need in the Real working World. Instruction on the most important skills follows:

HOW TO BROWN-NOSE

Because most companies do not give extra credit for reports plagiarized from *National Geographic*, brown-nosing is far more complex in the Real World than it was in college. To move up, you've got to suck up. If you are sexually repressed, however, kiss ass as follows:

1. *Agree with everything boss says, especially when you don't agree with it.*

EXAMPLE: "And I thought *I* was the only Rush Limbaugh fan around here!"

2. *Solicit advice from boss, especially when you don't want it.*

EXAMPLE: "What would *you* do with the rest of your life if you were me?"

3. *Solicit praise from boss, especially when you don't deserve it.*

EXAMPLE: "Um . . . yes, of course I am the one who color-coded the supply room to help prevent theft. I sure stayed late *that* night!"

4. *Compliment boss, especially when you don't mean it.*

EXAMPLE: "That wide polyester tie goes great with those white orthopedic shoes!"

5. *Dress like boss, especially when you have lost all shame.*

EXAMPLE: Wide polyester tie; white orthopedic shoes.

Pop Quiz

ARE YOU LIVING IN THE REAL WORLD?

1. Have you ever rented a car?
2. Do you save old clothes to be used as rags?
3. Have you ever washed the inside of your kitchen trash can?
4. Have you, in the past month, experienced brief yet disturbing flashes of maternal/paternal instinct?
5. Do you own a colander?

HOW TO LOOK BUSY

Generally, this will not be a concern until you are promoted to an executive position. But once you've created the illusion that you serve even the slightest purpose at your place of "business," there's no telling how far you'll go. In the Real working World, productivity is all a matter of appearances.

APPEARANCE. You are furiously taking notes while conducting an important telephone marketing survey.

REALITY. You are pretending to take notes while talking to your friend who has called collect from Bulgaria.

APPEARANCE. You are on the phone with a client in New York and you have said: "Yes, sirree! That stock is about to shoot through the roof, now's a great time to buy, I tell ya!"

REALITY. You are on the phone with a friend in Guam and you have said: "Yeah, this job totally sucks and my boss uses that spray paint on his bald sp . . . Yes, sirree! That stock is about to shoot through the roof, now's a great time to buy, I tell ya!"

APPEARANCE. You are at your computer writing a serious business memorandum to your department supervisor.

REALITY. You are at your computer telling dead-baby jokes to your E-mail correspondent in Namibia.

APPEARANCE. You are urgently plugging numbers into a complicated spreadsheet.

REALITY. You are playing Tetris.

APPEARANCE. You are staring at an empty computer screen, absorbed in deep thought.

REALITY. You have pressed "Escape" just in time, erasing a MacDraw portrait entitled *Supervisor with Pitchfork Wound*.

APPEARANCE. You are tapping away on calculator keys, helping out the accounting department.

REALITY. You are paying your electric bill.

APPEARANCE. You are reading the DOS manual.

REALITY. You are reading the *TV Guide* you have placed inside the DOS manual.

HOW TO DO YOUR JOB

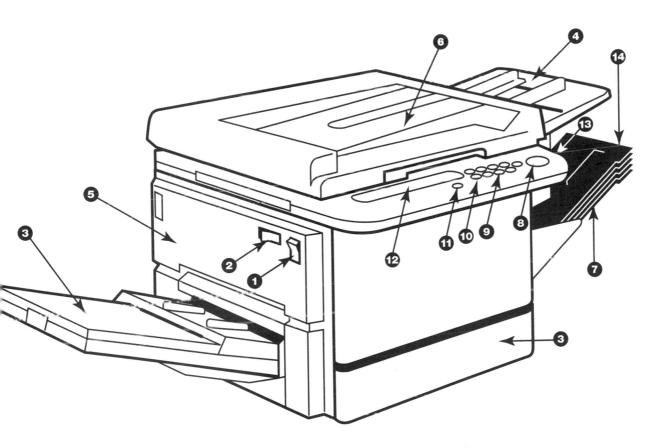

1	power switch	**8**	start copy button
2	power saver switch	**9**	reduction/enlargement control (REC)
3	paper tray	**10**	2-sided copy button
4	side document feeder (SDF)	**11**	copy quality adjustment
5	finisher door	**12**	graphic display
6	automatic document handler (ADH)	**13**	recirculating document handler (RDH)
7	sorter/collater	**14**	document output tray

XEROX[11] ETIQUETTE

There is nothing more distasteful than the rude Xeroxer. These crass copiers shove to the front of the line, do their business with the lid *up*, and race off with no regard for common copy courtesy. Such behavior is unbecoming in the Working Lifer. For you, the copy machine will become a second home. Treat your fellow Xeroxers as house guests. Tell them to call before stopping by. Ask them to bring beer.

Below, you will find answers to all your most pressing Xerox etiquette quandaries:

Q: What is the polite thing to say when I have 600 pages to Xerox for my violently insane boss and somebody else is using the machine?
A: The courteous comment is: "Can I *jump in*? I only have *one.*"

Q: Is there any sort of decorum as to who may *"jump in"* once I have begun Xeroxing 600 pages for my violently insane boss?
A: Everyone except the intern may jump in when you are Xeroxing.

Q: What is the honorable course of action when two Lifers arrive at the machine simultaneously to Xerox 600 pages for their violently insane bosses?
A: Both parties must turn to each other and politely say, *"Are you going to be a while?"* The better liar may proceed.

Q: What is the appropriate dress for Xeroxing?
A: A lead apron draped casually about the waist will absorb lingering radiation, while a short—yet straight—jacket fashionably prevents self-inflicted wounds.

Q: Is it considered poor form to Xerox invitations, comics, and other personal items during business hours?
A: It is considered poor form only when the party in question is not you.

Q: Is it considered mannerly to Xerox one's buttocks during business hours?
A: This, of course, depends on the nature of one's business.

Q: Several employees at my place of business enjoy mimicking the *Saturday Night Live* character who says, "Makin' copies; copy-o-ramas; copies, copies, copies." What is the recommended protocol?
A: The appropriate response is to clasp these individuals firmly yet politely by the neck, place them face side down on the Xerox glass, and close the lid. Reduce, duplicate, and discard original.

Q: What is the proper reply when one is asked, *"Do you know how to fix this?"*
A: The proper reply is: *"No."*

---

[11] *Reminder: In the Real working World, the office copy machine is* always *the "Xerox" machine, regardless of brand.*

HOW TO NOT FIX THE XEROX MACHINE

Even the most productive office comes to a complete, grinding standstill when something goes wrong with the Xerox machine. That is precisely why it is so important that you never attempt to fix it.

There are many additional hazards involved in Xerox repair. You could develop a reputation as the only employee who not only knows what toner *is*, but how and where to add it; or, you might become the resident interpreter of frightening flashing pictograms. To help you get less familiar with the tool of your trade, we now turn to the . . .

XEROX "NO TROUBLE"-SHOOTING GUIDE

TROUBLE	INDICATION	SOLUTION
Paper tray is empty	*threatening beeping sound; frightening flashing pictogram*	*Walk away; return in 10 minutes.*
Needs toner	*frightening flashing pictogram*	*Walk away; return in 10 minutes.*
Paper jam	*machine stops & retains original document*	*Walk away; return in 10 minutes with intern.*
Your boss is violently insane	*You have been asked to sort, stack, and staple 600 double-sided copies of the New Testament.*	*Place your résumé under lid, set for 600 copies, walk away; return in 10 hours.*
Machine is working perfectly	*You are sorting, stacking, and stapling 600 double-sided copies of the New Testament for your violently insane boss.*	*Accidentally sprinkle box of paper clips into rotary mechanism, place Out of Order sign on lid, walk away.*
You are becoming violently insane	*You have started taking pride in your Xerox prowess.*	*Run away.*

MANAGING YOUR BOSS

The most important lesson any Working Lifer can learn from a supervisor is how not to supervise. This lesson is easily reinforced through "discussion sections" or "lab groups" with trustworthy cubemates. Whenever your boss is out, assemble in the conference room, order a pizza, and tear your supervisor to shreds the way each of you normally does in the privacy of your own home. Bring the following profiles to your next lab session for a lively interaction:

THE CONTROL FREAK

PROFESSIONAL PROFILE: These supervisors are easily identified by three traits:

1. They do not let you do anything.
2. Anything they do let you do, they make you do again.
3. Then they do it "correctly."

Control Freaks cannot stop themselves from redecorating your cube, resetting your margins, and rethinking your thoughts ("Are you sure you want to reduce that page by forty percent instead of thirty-nine and seventeen-thousandths percent?") You'll know they are working to potential once they achieve a complete Control Freakout. This entails plastering every piece of office machinery[12] with the following sign: ABSOLUTELY NO ONE BUT ME IS AUTHORIZED TO TOUCH THIS PIECE OF OFFICE MACHINERY.—C.F.

MANAGEMENT TECHNIQUE: To properly manage the Control Freak, you must understand his or her philosophy of work delegation: "If you want the job done right, do it yourself." It is only through hysterical pleading that the Freaks relinquish any responsibility, such as allowing you to make them a 1:27 lunch reservation at the second booth in the back room of Chez Snooté—which they will change as soon as you hang up.

To motivate these managers, try writing them a standard "suicide memo" and they may even permit you to do something related to your job. Your new duties will always be presented as *very* important responsibilities:

FREAK: I've been thinking. It's high time someone really demonstrated leadership skills and started pulling apart all the Jumbo Gem paper clips I've seen clumped together around here. Think you're ready for the challenge?

LIFER: I'll certainly give it my best shot, C.F.

FREAK: There's a lot riding on this project, as far as your career goes. It's a *very* important responsibility.

LIFER: I'll get right on it as soon as you uncuff me from your wrist, C.F.

12 *except the hidden camera above your desk*

In time, Control Freaks may be groomed into managers who trust you with interesting, stimulating projects. And in time, you are going to frolic through the forest with Casper the Friendly Ghost.

THE TUTOR

PROFESSIONAL PROFILE: The Tutors think you are retarded. That is why they hired you. They long to be your mentor; your friend; your role model. They remember what it was like when *they* were struggling Entry-Level Lifers. If they were normal managers, they would have blocked this experience out of their memories long ago.

In their friendly, condescending way, Tutors feel the need to teach you everything about your job.[13] Each lesson is preceded by the word "now," as in: "Now. Here is how we staple," or: "Now. It is time for us to learn to tie a double knot." Unwilling just to teach you what to do, they must also teach you *why*. "Now," they say. "The reason why we staple is so that things stick together."

Many Tutors eventually assume a parental role, an obvious mistake. Extending their tutelage from the professional (stapling) to the personal (spermicide), they offer advice on the most embarrassing facets of your private life. These lessons are preceded by the phrase, "If you ever want to talk . . ." This phrase translates in the Real World to: "*I* want to talk."

More than anything, Tutors want to be your buddy. That is why they'll stop by your cube each Friday at 4:59, generously share more of their work with you, and cheerfully say: "Don't stay too late, it's Friday!" Then they'll go home.

MANAGEMENT TECHNIQUE: Managing the Tutor can be rewarding if you take the time to absorb his or her wisdom. Once thirty seconds are up, continue acting mentally challenged or you may lose your job. Follow this simple rule: *When the Tutor starts with "Now," you respond with "Oh!"*

[13] *usually incorrectly*

For example: "Oh! I did not realize that these staples came attached in long rows," or: "Oh! I did not realize that babies were not delivered by storks."

As long as you pretend the Tutors know more than you, they will remain loyal, productive managers. But use this technique with discretion. In the Real working World, promotions are given out to the *mildly*—not the *severely*—retarded.

THE DODDERING DEADWOOD

PROFESSIONAL PROFILE: Like their antique manual typewriters, the Doddering Deadwoods are both decorative and obsolete. Sporting silver manes and historical wardrobes; their primary function is to be dusted off and displayed to shareholders as evidence of corporate staying power. Immediately upon waking up, they are placed back in cold storage.

Deadwoods' method of business communication is stream of consciousness. They refer to you as (a) "my apprentice" or (b) "someone who is here to fix the elevator." Although they are unaware of any advances in the workplace since the polio vaccine, they are still not impaired from getting the job done. After all, that is what you were hired to do.

Facing extinction in today's heavily logged workplace, the Deadwood is being uprooted by a crop of new-growth "temporary consultants."[14] Once supplanted, the Deadwood will rely on his or her unique qualifications to land a job as a college career counselor.

MANAGEMENT TECHNIQUE: There is much to be learned by working with aged and seasoned Deadwoods, but do not expect them to learn it all at once. Begin with something simple, like overnight mail. After you explain seventy thousand times how to fill out the Federal Express form, Deadwoods demonstrate mastery by stating the following: "How do you fill out the Federal Express form?"

Another skill to tackle is basic faxing ("wiring" in Deadwood dialectic). "Face up or

[14] *a.k.a. "permanent replacements"*

face down?" is their most frequent question—so frequent that many Working Lifers are tempted to verbalize the colorful responses they've dreamed up over time. This is ill advised. It is your unspoken responsibility to overlook this supervisor's brazen incompetency and make him or her feel less like a doddering old bat. Teach the Deadwood to use a push-button phone instead.

What makes these managers tick? A pacemaker—so avoid putting them in stressful situations. Lessons at the copy ("mimeograph") machine will be fruitless, yet amusing when they confuse it with the paper shredder. It is a mistake of irrevocable proportions to introduce any device resembling a computer ("magic box") into Deadwood environs.

Motivating these managers requires a classic hands-off approach. For you to do their job efficiently, the less they know, the better.

DER SÜPERVISOR

PROFESSIONAL PROFILE: They goose-step down the hall each morning at 0:800 hours. As the click of their heels grows louder, sweat begins soaking your desk blotter. They arrive at your cube to deploy the day's work orders. As always, these are both arbitrary and contradictory:

"What time did you punch in today, Lifer!"

"At 0:500 hours, Süpervisor!"

"How do you account for the time you have frittered away since then, Lifer!"

"I have Xeroxed the Yellow Pages as you commanded, Süpervisor!"

"I commanded you to Xerox the White Pages!"

"I am not worthy, Süpervisor!"

Der Süpervisors consider their jobs a mere stepping-stone to world domination. They consider you the stone upon which they most enjoy stepping. Lacking interpersonal skills beyond "rude" and "abusive," they scream at you whenever they crash their computers and fire you several times a day. But first, they march you out to the water cooler so your colleagues won't miss anything.

When Der Süpervisors are not tapping phone conversations, counting pens in the supply closet, or clocking your lunch break, they are placing perverted classified ads of this sort:

> *Dom. Slvdrvr. sks. Submisv Masocst 4 hot humiliation.*

These ads are placed in the Help Wanted section, not the Personals.

MANAGEMENT TECHNIQUE: To improve your working relationship with Der Süpervisors, take the GREs immediately. Then legally change your name and city of residence.

THE BIONIC BOOMER

PROFESSIONAL PROFILE: These megalomanagers have everything: condos in superior neighborhoods, kids in superior play groups, marriages in superior court. How do they "do it all" while you barely have the strength to remove the plastic film from your dinner tray each night? By farming out their private lives to freelance help and concentrating on something far more lucrative: their careers. When they combine this with the ulcer medication, psychoanalysis, and cocaine addiction, these bosses become bionic.

Being bionic, they are also creatures of artificial intelligence.[15] Instead of actual work experience, they are programmed with highly irrelevant data received in MBA management training programs. This technology allows

[15] *and tans*

them to catapult to the top without working up from the bottom, the way human employees do. Equipped with no idea how things get done in a real office, they practice a "virtual reality" style of management that assumes you, too, are a machine:

BOOMER (without irony): Do you have a couple minutes?

YOU: Are you kidding?

BOOMER: No, I am not. I need you to make mailing labels for the general population of the continental United States. How long do you think it will take? Ten minutes?

As supervisors, the Boomers' greatest strength is a snappy style of dress. Females go in for the Sexy Librarian look—prim without being proper—while male counterparts opt for Armani power suits and ambitious attempts at Steven Segal–style ponytails. Thus disguised, they engage in daily robotics as if everything is under control.

MANAGEMENT TECHNIQUE: Getting the most from bionic bosses is as simple as understanding they are one step away from a short circuit at all times. This is especially true ever since they quit smoking and went on "the patch." Remember, Boomers appear superhuman on the surface, but their lives have spun completely out of control. The observant Lifer detects the nastily chewed fingernails; the premature wrinkles; the deep sobbing sounds.

Like Steve Austin and Jamie Somers before them, these bionic individuals live in fear that someone will discover they are only a simulation. To avoid tripping a wire, manage them in a *completely nonthreatening manner*. Show them that you are capable, but not *too* capable. Reassure them that they're doing a terrific job at work and the Nicaraguan nanny they've hired to raise darling little Lucifer and Jezebel is doing a terrific job at home. Tell them you've noticed an improvement in their Chronic Fatigue Syndrome since they started chugging that hazelnut-Mylanta espresso you've been serving them each day. Above all, do not remind them that the '80s are over.

THE UN-BOSS

PROFESSIONAL PROFILE: Un-bosses suffer an advanced form of scoliosis in which they lose their spines completely. Often triggered by fear of their own bosses, symptoms include: running into your cube every five minutes for advice on projects you know[16] nothing about, making sure all their decisions are first made by you, and insisting that others take advantage of them. Motivated by a profound sense of insecurity, they also suck their thumbs when no one is looking. Un-bosses never aspired to managerial positions; they just found themselves there one day. Consequently, they do not direct, manage, or lead you. They prefer you to direct, manage, and lead them. As long as they can take all the credit.

MANAGEMENT TECHNIQUE: It is advisable to pull these supervisors aside and tactfully explain why you must let them go. Then replace them with a proven leader who deserves an enormous raise. Be sure to notify personnel of your promotion.

[16] *and care*

BASIC WORKPLACE COMMUNICATION

To become proficient in this area, it will be necessary to forget everything you learned about effective communication in your college Mass Comm. classes.

See how long *that* took? That's about how long it will take to become an effective communicator in the Real working World, too. Here are the basics:

Never talk in person when you can talk on the phone, never talk on the phone when you can send a fax, never send a fax when you can send a memo, never send a memo when you can send E-mail, never send E-mail when you can send a temp, never send a temp when you can send an intern.

In cases where human interaction is absolutely unavoidable, it must take place only in unruly groups of noncommunicative and incoherent individuals who will reduce the risk of anyone's communicating anything to anyone else. *Never have a conversation when you can have a meeting.*

BEATING MEETINGS

The ideal meeting is one at which you are not present. Sure, you may be slaving away right now while everyone is at some important meeting you were not invited to with some important people you were not introduced to. But if you're slaving away so much, where are you finding time to read this book? And if you went to meetings all day, where would you find time to finish it? So kiss those crazy meeting dreams goodbye and do something productive, like calling your friend in Finland and reading aloud the previous passage.

In the unlikely event that you are asked to attend, never say anything logical during meetings. This is easiest if you work in the communications field, which often forbids Lifers from saying anything at all during meetings. If forced to sit in on the ironically named "brainstorming" meeting, say especially moronic things. For example, if you are supposed to be brainstorming ideas to promote an important new brand of steel wool pads, a good suggestion would be: *"I feel it is essential to plant chrysanthemums before the first frost of the season."* Otherwise you risk standing out. Worse, you risk impressing someone. Then you will be forced to attend more meetings, and your long-distance read-aloud time will suffer.

If there is one meeting to avoid more than any other, it is the "weekly meeting." These affairs are so named because they tend to start bright and early Monday morning (reason enough to call in sick) and drag on for the rest of the week (reason enough to call in dead). Being dead would certainly have a detrimental effect upon your ability to read aloud.

It is not professional to go into any meeting unprepared. Always bring a pen and notepad so you may draw unflattering caricatures of your boss and pass them to colleagues who have not yet slipped into a coma. Fax these to your Finnish friend once you're done with the book.

MEMO CONTROL

It is an unwritten rule of corporate communication that everyone has to write memos, but no one has to read them. It is best that this rule remains unwritten. Otherwise, it could become a memo, and then how would people find out about it?

To eliminate the possibility of anyone reading your memos, be sure they are at least three pages long, single spaced, and mildly snippy in tone. From there, follow the standard format of those stored in your garbage can:

1. CHOOSE AN IDENTITY. Type the name of the person who won't be reading the memo, and whoever you claim to be. Use cryptic initials to confuse readers early on. Some memo scribes add in handwritten initials later, apparently to prevent widespread memo fraud. You should do the same, but only when you are forging a signature.

2. CHOOSE A TOPIC. Always pick one your reader cares nothing about.

3. ABBREVIATE WILDLY. Apply what you learned in step one re: initials. Why use full words when you can cut time and comprehension in half with indecipherable shorthand?

4. USE OFFICIAL-SOUNDING LANGUAGE. If you must use full words, make sure they would sound very impressive if anyone knew what they meant.

Based on our model, here is the kind of masterful memo that's sure to be ignored:

MEMORANDUM

To: XYZ
Fr: E-LL *E-LL*
Re: *MY RAISE*[17]

X:
Cn U pls. mt. w/me re: $? As U no,
it has been brought 2 my
attention, per se, that
necessitating implementation of
ancillary compensation is 2b
facilitated, as it were, ev. 6
mos. I.e, I m ovrdu 2 ascertain
my erstwhile prfmnc rvw., etc.
Pneumonoultramicroscopic-
silicovolcanoconiosis.
Status quo, et al, in toto, too.
S.A.S.E./BYOB

As such,

Thnx!!

E *E*

cc: REM, CVS, PCP

---

[17] *see rule 2, above*

PHONE MANNERISMS
The first step in developing a businesslike phone manner is to untangle the cord. Read the foolproof directions below when you are at the office, so you can follow along instead of doing work:

Pick up the receiver and remove the jack that connects to the base. Now, stand on your chair. Go on, stand. Okay, grasping the end of the cord in one hand and the receiver in the other, drop the receiver and let it dangle. See it spinning round and round? That means it's working! Once spinning has terminated, plug the jack back into the phone. Sit.

You are now ready to demonstrate a businesslike phone manner:

1. HOW TO HANG UP ON SOMEONE
(a) Turn the Tables.
You are on an important call with your mother. Suddenly, your date from last night calls on the other line.

wrong: "I have to get back to work, Mom."

right: "Well, Mom, I'll let you get back to work."

(b) Whisper
You are on an important call with your roommate. Suddenly, you become unbearably bored.

wrong: "Look, I really can't talk now."

right: (whispering) "Look, I really can't talk now."

(c) Attempt to set up a conference call.

2. HOW TO BE PLEASANT

wrong: "Dad, I told you! I can't pay you back until I get a raise!"

right: "Mom, it's been great talking to you! Say hi to Dad for me! Bye!"

HELPFUL REAL WORLD TIP!

Memo Don't
When presented with miscellaneous clippings and other flammables marked "read, initial, and circulate," ignore the first and last commands but scrupulously obey the second. This will help your colleagues resist the temptation to inscribe little sunshines or sentiments such as "Back at ya!" next to your name. Any colleague who does not understand this concept (a) must be avoided at lunch and (b) is going to ask you to lunch. Plus, they are going to ask you to Friendly's, where you will have to order a Rutti-tooti-puffin-spoof-awich with a person who does not think it is funny.

3. HOW TO USE YOUR VOICE MAIL

wrong: Read the 600-page manual.

right: "Hi, I'm either on the other line or away from my desk. This machine does not take messages."

EVERYTHING YOU EVER WANTED TO KNOW ABOUT SEX HARASSMENT

An increasingly popular mode of workplace communication is sexual harassment. First legalized by Supreme Court Justice Clarence Thomas in 1992, this method is still relatively new, resulting in occasional double entendres or misconstrued body language. Unfortunately, sexual harassment does not follow a standard format, as does the memo, so it is often difficult to tell if you are engaged in it at all. The guide below will help you communicate more clearly, whether you are giving or receiving.

CONCISE SEXUAL HARASSMENT

NONSEXUAL HARASSMENT	POSSIBLE SEXUAL HARASSMENT	HARASSMENT
"Yolanda, can I see you privately in my cube, please?"	"Yolanda, I'd love to see you privately in my cube."	"Yo, I'd love to see your privates in my cube."
"That is a nice dress you are wearing."	"That dress is very flattering to your figure."	"Nice hooters!"
pubic hair on Coke	pubic hair on cream soda	pubic hair on reproductive organ
"I need you to type that report in eight seconds."	"I need you."	"Do me."

OFFICE EXPLETIVES: THE TERRIBLE 20

Once they've sold their souls to the corporate machine, many Working Lifers feel the occasional need to regain some semblance of humanity. One way to salvage a shred of self-respect is to censor your workplace vocabulary. Before speaking, ask yourself: *"Would I ever use this word or phrase outside the office?"* Answer yourself: *"No, and I promise I will not use it inside the office either."* The following foul language must never pass the lips of the Working Lifer:

swamped	regroup	interface
telephone tag	make a	in the loop
FYI	mental note	mental health day
r&d	up to speed	touch base
guesstimate	feedback	go to bat for
generate	input	stepped away
downtime	in-house	Big *Cajones*

IRREGULAR CONJUGATIONS OF WORKPLACE PROFANITIES

The following words and phrases are obscene only when used in the context described below:

take: (verb) something that is done to a meeting.

ballpark: (verb) something that is done to an estimated dollar amount.

catch-up: (noun) something that is played.

do: (verb) something that is done to lunch.

housecleaning:[18] (noun) something that is done to a staff.

cc: (verb) something that is done to the receiver of a duplicated correspondence.

live: (adj) something that a file is.

Ciao: (noun) something that is said by non-Italian employees

TGIF: something that is said by any employee who is not abbreviating a 1978 movie starring Donna Summer.

[18] *remember: "Would I ever use this word or phrase outside the office?"*

MORALE BOOSTERS: PEP RALLIES OF THE REAL WORLD

Occasionally in the Real working World, things become less . . . electrifying than usual. It is at these times that a special wacky tie week or Dunkin' Munchkin Monday can provide just the lift the gang needs, especially if management frowns upon mercy killings.

Office softball games, picnics, and illegal worksite gambling all bring the staff together as one big family. Therefore, you are expected to act appropriately dysfunctional. Suppose there's an exciting baby pool under way and you're asked to bet money on whether Muriel in customer relations will have a boy or girl. Play along. Don't dwell on the fact that Muriel in customer relations miscarried the last time the staff took bets on her pregnancy. Instead, make it worth good old Muriel's while to leak you the results of her ultrasound. Tell her you'll give her a cut of the $7.36 booty.

And remember how much you enjoyed family vacations? You can have even more fun with your new "work family" on a weekend corporate retreat. Designed to strengthen trust and teamwork, activities will include blindfolding colleagues and leading them through the forest while discussing third-quarter profit strategy. Now what could be more enjoyable than that?[19]

There are countless ways the listless Lifer can gain a fresh perspective. But all of these pale in comparison to the mother of all morale boosters, the office party.

OFFICE PARTY POLITICS

HOW TO HAVE FUN AT THE COMPANY CHRISTMAS PARTY

Do not be alarmed by the company Christmas party. This is the event your colleagues have been waiting for all year. That is because they have not gone out socially since the Christmas party last year.

The Christmas party gives your coworkers a rare chance to wear suggestive clothing, drink 80-proof eggnog, and lambada the night away. Throw caution to the wind and join the fun. Look! There's mousy little Gladys freebasing in the corner with the payroll guy! And, hey! Isn't that stuffy old Eugene snake-dancing with a lampshade on his head? Oh, the stories you'll tell tomorrow morning, when your supervisors have nearly forgotten the disgusting propositions they whispered to you all night. Why not refresh their memory and ask your secret Santas for a Christmas bonus to make the season bright?

HOW TO HAVE FUN AT THE OFFICE BABY SHOWER

To ensure a good time at the baby shower, stay home. Attendance will only encourage the expectant mother to bring her spawn to work once she has it removed.

HOW TO HAVE FUN AT THE OFFICE BIRTHDAY PARTY

The real fun of the office birthday party is not

[19] *besides leaving them there*

the special, barely defrosted, plain Sara Lee sponge cake purchased seconds earlier from the SpeedyMart next door. It's not those 14.6 minutes everyone spends not eating the cake, but looking at their watches and worrying about all the calls they will miss until the celebration finally stops. It's not even that warm feeling the birthday boy or girl gets when he or she is eventually left sitting all alone with a party hat and a gift certificate for a small Sankaspresso at Tasty Pastry. Certainly, these things are all fun. But the *real* fun of the office birthday party is the office birthday card.

HOW TO SIGN THE OFFICE BIRTHDAY CARD

Many Working Lifers become stress-ridden when forced to sign the company birthday card. First, they are uncomfortable with the clandestine nature of the event, worried that the honoree will sneak into their cube just as they are removing the card from the sealed manila envelope in which it is safeguarded. Then they feel pressured to write something clever and original. The solution is a boldly colored Flair pen. No matter what you write, it is far more interesting in green. If you are still "blocked," use one of the approaches below to get those creative juices flowing:

1. Create a Job-Related Pun. The card is for Euell in public affairs. How about: "I hope *Euell* Have a Hot *Public Affair* on Your Birthday!"

2. Lie. The card is for Dick, your cubemate. Write: "Dick, it sure has been great having you for a cubemate!"

3. Tell Them Not to Have Fun. The card is for Inez in bookkeeping. Why not: "Inez, don't party *too* much!"

4. Write ''Ditto!'' Above Whatever the Last Person Wrote. The card is for Inez in bookkeeping. Why not: "Ditto!"

5. Play Off the Illustration on the Card. The card is for Frank in marketing. Try: "Frank, If You Eat Too Much Cake, You'll Look Like These Hippos!"

6. ''Ditto!''

7. Write the Words ''Happy, Happy!'' The card is for a person who makes you very angry, angry.

8. Write ''Cheers!'' The card is for a person you have never heard of.

HOW NOT TO SIGN THE OFFICE BIRTHDAY CARD

* note: the headless, '90s-style smiley face is considered equally inappropriate.

THE PERFORMANCE REVIEW: YOUR ENTRY-LEVEL REPORT CARD

In the Real working World, you know you are doing a good job if you haven't been fired yet. Still, many Working Lifers are used to getting graded, so they foolishly wonder if the boss has any opinion whatsoever about the quality of their work. A performance review meeting can be the report card you're looking for. What's more, it's one your parents will never find.

PERFORMANCE REHEARSAL. To ensure a successful meeting, practice acting like an em-

ployee who is not entirely without virtue. Set the stage early with one of the following strategies, both designed to show the boss how much you deserve a raise.

(a) Show the boss how poor you are. Several weeks before the review, hang a sign on the bulletin board that says, *WANTED: Apartment. Can Afford No More than $50/mo.* As review day approaches, replace the sign with: *WANTED. Canned Goods.* Start wearing tattered clothing to work. Ask your supervisor if you can borrow money "to get home." On review day, do not eat. This will cause your stomach to growl throughout the meeting. It will also prevent you from throwing up once it is over.

(b) Show the boss how valuable you are. Several weeks before the review, hang a sign on the bulletin board that says, *WANTED: Home Office Computer. Will Pay Any Price for Chance to Do Additional Work on My Own Time.* As review day approaches, replace the sign with: *WANTED: Additional Work.* Start wearing suits to make your boss think you are interviewing for other jobs. On review day, say you are "considering several interesting offers." This will cause your boss to growl throughout the meeting. It will not, however, prevent you from throwing up once it is over.

PERFORMANCE ANXIETY. It is normal to be somewhat jittery or slightly paralyzed with terror the first time you engage in performance review relations. These feelings often subside once the review is postponed eight or nine times. By then, however, your craving to be stroked by the boss may have grown so strong that you risk getting jerked around. This results in premature evaluation:

BOSS: "We think you're doing such a fantastic job, we've decided to give you less money."

YOU: "Did you say *fantastic job?!* Wow! How much less can I get??!"

It's okay. This happens to many Entry-Level employees their first time. It doesn't make you any less a Lifer. With experience, you'll learn to better satisfy your needs: You'll make up some accomplishments to boast about. You'll make up some objectives to attain. Eventually, you'll turn into a real hustler and the boss will offer top dollar for your services. At this point, inform him or her that you are not *that* kind of hustler.

KNOWING WHAT YOU WANT. What you want out of your performance review is money.

Ask for a cost-of-living increase retroactive to the year the review was originally scheduled. Once that is postponed, take a long shot. Ask for minimum wage.

KNOWING WHAT YOUR BOSS WANTS. Good negotiators put themselves in the other person's shoes during a performance review. God only knows where your boss's shoes have been. Therefore, it is better to try to determine what he or she is thinking. Here is what he or she is thinking:

- Look, there is my employee.
- I am going to commend my employee for doing a good job.
- I am not going to give my employee a raise.

The reason your boss is not going to give you a raise is: (a) the "salary freeze"; (b) the "company-wide percentage[20] that *all* employees are getting this year," or (c) the fact that you are doing a good job. You are not, however, doing a *great* job. What about the day you had a run in your stocking?[21] Or that time your father died?

GETTING TO NO. It may appear that you will leave your performance review with nothing more than you had going in. This is fallacious. Instead of money, most employers are willing to compensate you with a generous increase in work and an inflated job title.

To summarize, we see that the successful performance review will land the shrewd Working Lifer in one of the following three situations:

1. THE WIN/LOSE SITUATION: new title/more work

2. THE LOSE/LOSE SITUATION: same title/more work

3. THE WIN/WIN SITUATION: acute vomiting/worker's comp

---

[20] *0%*

[21] *particularly if you are male*

The Fear of Being Found Out

Many Working Lifers worry that they'll be exposed for the impostors they really are. To find out if you are plagued by this not unreasonable phobia, take the following personality test:

When I am sitting in my cube working, I feel
(a) dehydrated
(b) like strolling up to the roof and opening fire on a group of innocent passersby
(c) certain that the president of the company is going to walk in any minute and tell me to clean out my desk because I do not have the slightest idea what I am doing.

If you answered (c), you suffer from the Fear of Being Found Out. Chances are, you've recently changed the message on your answering machine from: *Hey, Dudes and Bettys, we're too tripped out of our minds to get the phone right now, so we'll call you back when it stops breathing,* to: *Please leave the date, time, and a brief message after the tone, and we shall be pleased to return your call.*[22] You've done this "just in case anyone from work calls."

SYMPTOMS. The Fear of Being Found Out manifests itself early in your professional life, generally the moment you hear the words "You're hired." Some victims believe the speaker has confused them with a qualified applicant. Others think they'll show up the first day and discover that the boss really said, "You're tired."

Left unchecked, the condition peaks during your first business trip. Here, you try desperately to look older (granny glasses, giant briefcase) so colleagues won't mistake you for a fifth-grader participating in "career day." This is complicated by the fact that the last time you took a trip, you tried desperately to look younger (propeller beanie, giant lollipop) so airline personnel would not mistake you for an Entry-Level Lifer using an expired college ID to scam a student fare.

The following scenarios also indicate that you suffer the Fear:

1. You inadvertently set the burglar alarm off at work and become convinced that everyone will think you were trying to break in to steal the computers.[23]

2. You tell your parents *never* to leave messages from "Mom" or "Dad" for fear that the receptionist will discover you were not immaculately conceived from some enormous professional organization.

3. When leaving messages for friends at work, you add "Mr." or "Mrs." to your name because you suspect that they, too, suffer the Fear.

4. You clam up when a colleague asks, "So where were you before this job?" because the real answer is "At a frat party."

[22] *Reminder: When using your answering machine, always instruct callers to leave messages after the tone. Otherwise, they will not know.*
[23] *when all you were really after was a box of floppys*

CAUSES. Many who suffer the Fear are verbally abused in the early stages of their careers, branded with the following derogatory terms:

low man on the totem pole   wet behind the ears
green   unseasoned
tenderfoot   punk

Combined, we see that victims learn to view themselves as small, wooden, green men suffering from fallen arches and ear secretions because they are childish, bland hoodlums.
    Is it any wonder they don't want to be found out?

RECOVERY. To aid the healing process, you must begin to think of yourself as the professional you truly are. First, become delusionary. Next, take a deep, cleansing breath and study the self-esteem exercise below.

HOW TO PRETEND YOU ARE NOT A FRAUD

You're Not	You Are
a washroom attendant at Merrill Lynch	*with* Merrill Lynch
a baby-sitter	*in* early childhood education
a secretary	*on* the support side
on unemployment	*between* projects
a waiter	in "the service industry"
a house painter	in "the arts"
a good-for-nothing lazy drifting bum lacking any sense of commitment or motivation to do anything productive with your pathetic excuse for a life	a "consultant"

SECTION **IV**

Entry-Level Finances

A Super-Scientific, Double-Blind-Tested, Exhaustively Researched, Conclusively Proven Plan for Effective Money Management:

SECTION

V

Entry-Level Social Life

YOUR NEW SOCIAL LIFE:
some assembly required

Finding Entry-Level friends requires effort. No longer are you sequestered on an idyllic campus with scores of other young scholars who share your taste in literature, art, and infomercials. No longer do all your friends eat, shower, and sleep together. Not since you decided to keep things platonic, anyway.

When making new friends, remember: Unlike college, everyone in the Real social World does not already know one another. It is often necessary to introduce yourself. "Greetings," you might say. "My name is Otto. Would you like to be friends?" Using this technique, you'll meet loads of other Social Lifers in no time, though it may take a while to get used to being called Otto.

Do not be intimidated by meeting others without the benefit of a built-in social life. Instead, cultivate stimulating new friendships with the kinds of people you never met on your homogeneous old college campus. The kinds of people who have entirely different interests and values from your own. One option is to call all your old friends from high school, but certainly there are many others.

FRIENDS FROM WORK:
At first, you may be hesitant to befriend anyone at work. They seem so much older, so much stuffier, so much more . . . married. Are these really the kind of people who need to know you were up until two last night playing naked Trivial Pursuit? Then they would find out that you did not know the answer to the question "Which dance, according to the New York Safety Council, was the largest cause of back problems in 1961?" and your professional reputation would be sullied.[1]

As you become more desperate, you may meet someone at work with whom you identify. This person will probably also just be starting out, and will probably also have dark rings under both eyes. Ask this person if he or she would like to have lunch with you sometime. Slander your colleagues throughout the meal. You now have an official work friend.

Work friends can become *friend* friends only with the addition of alcohol. This will enable you to talk about things you would never talk about with someone you work with. Interesting approaches to board games, for example. Eventually, you may discover that *all* your friends are work friends. This is a sign that you have truly arrived in the Real social World. In no time at all, you've assembled all the camaraderie you'll need to schmooze your way to a better job.

OTHER PEOPLE'S FRIENDS:
It is best to shun other people's friends. You meet them through other people, and sud-

[1] *the Twist*

denly they think they are your best friend. They call you up three times a week though you never return a single call. They stop by unannounced when you are wearing slippers. They leave their jacket so they have to come back. This would be fine if they were anything like the other people who first introduced you.[2] But they are not. They are boring. They are so boring, you wonder what the other people see in them. What you don't realize is that the other people also think of them as other people's friends. They are happy to pawn them off on you.

It is especially important to avoid parties composed of other people's friends. In these situations, you will feel like you did the first week of college, when everyone but you seemed to know one another. By week's end, you finally made a few friends, most notably the hunchback captain of the calculus club and that girl with the beard. Don't make the same mistake twice.

There are those rare occasions when you will like other people's friends better than you like the other people themselves. You would be well advised to steal these friends and drop the other people like a hot potato. You never really liked calculus and facial hair anyway.

FRIENDS FROM HOBBY CLUBS, CIVIC SERVICE LEAGUES, AND BIBLE STUDY GROUPS:
Come on.

COUPLE FRIENDS:
Couple friends are valuable because they are two friends for the price of one, though certain couples require separate payment to be your friends at the same time. It is not difficult to meet couple friends in the Real social World. That is because you have embarked upon the coupling years. The coupling years are the years in which you find yourself making frequent reservations for parties of three, five, and seven.

Many couple friends had individual names and identities before you lost touch with them. For example, remember your old friend Mort and your old friend Selma? Now they are your new friend Mortandselma. Sometimes Mortandselma take on Mort's former personality. Sometimes Mortandselma take on Selma's former personality. Sometimes Mortandselma leave their apartment.

Couple friends come in several configurations:

a) those in which you like one member but not the other
b) those in which you like both members individually but not together
c) those in which you like both members together but not individually
d) those in which you do not like either member individually or together[3]

Of course, the best couples to befriend are those in configuration d. You will never have to worry about whether or not to invite them to the same party once they break up.

SINGLE FRIENDS:
What if you yourself are in a couple and you wish to cultivate more *single* friends? First, the two of you need to change your name to something less cumbersome than Mortandselma. How about Kris? That is a nice, simple name that is appropriately gender-free.

Kris, to cultivate single friends, be sensitive to their situation. Whenever they're in the same room, act as if they don't exist. Engage in public displays of affection with your mate, such as holding hands, hugging, placing your tongues in each other's bodily orifices, etc. If you are shy, another way to be sensitive to your single friends is to make them watch you fight with your mate. Bicker. Nag. Hurl a bottle of Southern Comfort across the room and scream, *"I gave up the best years of my life for you!"*

If you are sensitive to your single friends in this manner, they will be so sickened by your behavior that they'll be glad they don't have a partner of their own. Kris, you are a supportive and caring friend indeed.

Pop Quiz

ARE YOU LIVING IN THE REAL WORLD?

1. Do you have a "daily planner"?
2. Do you have a sugar bowl?
3. Have you ever purchased air freshener?
4. Are you careful to drink decaf after five p.m.?
5. Are there any three-way light bulbs in your apartment?

---

[2] *or you had not already sold the jacket*

[3] *Only in the Real social World is it possible to have friends you do not really like.*

NEW BEST FRIENDS:

If you are like most Social Lifers, you'll soon meet a new and trusty confidant who will always be there when you need a sympathetic ear.[4] Ideally, you'll want one who was referred by any number of your old best friends. Be choosy: Do you want a Freudian best friend, or a best friend with a behavioral approach? Are you looking for a temporary best friend to stop in on every few weeks, or a long-term best friend whom you can visit every day, sacking out on the office couch and reminiscing about your childhood? Whichever you decide, choose a best friend who charges on a sliding scale if your health insurance does not cover treatment by new best friends.

PSYCHIC FRIENDS:

By phoning the Psychic Friends Network, you will soon be socializing with the likes of Dionne Warwick and LaToya Jackson.

IMAGINARY FRIENDS:

These will be your closest friends in the Real social World.

ANATOMY OF A
REAL-WORLD
FRIENDSHIP

FIRST FRIEND: "Hi, Itzhak, it's Otto. Do you want to go out for a drink tomorrow night?"

Beeeeeep.

SECOND FRIEND: "Hi, Otto. I've got to work late tomorrow, but what about Wednesday?"

Beeeeeep.

FIRST FRIEND: "Wednesday's no good. Mortandselma are coming over, and you know what *they're* like together. Next week sometime?"

Beeeeeep.

SECOND FRIEND: "I'm out of town next week. I'm free the third Saturday in October. Does that work for you?"

Beeeeep.

FIRST FRIEND: "October's booked solid. Are you busy in 1997?"

Beeeep.

SECOND FRIEND: "Only Dionne and LaToya will know for sure. I'll call them for a reading and get back to you."

Beeeep.

FIRST FRIEND: click. dial tone.

Beeeeep.

SECOND FRIEND: click. dial tone.

Beeeeep.

THIRD FRIEND: "Hi, Itzhak, my name is Simon, I'm a friend of Otto's. Otto tells me we're just *so* alike and I was wondering if you want to get together sometime. Have you ever backpacked through Yugoslavia? . . ."

---

[4] *except Wednesdays when he or she is playing golf*

The "None of My New Friends Are as Cool as My Old Friends" Syndrome

After acquiring some new friends, you may be frustrated to find that you don't feel as close to them as you do your old friends. It does not occur to you that this is because you have known them for four days instead of four years. Instead, you surmise that they are simply not as "cool."

In a misguided attempt to rectify the problem, you subconsciously seek out new friends who remind you of old friends. Eventually, you become a poor judge of character, as evidenced by the following thought process:

- "My old friend Itzhak once backpacked across Yugoslavia."
- "My new friend Simon once backpacked across Yugoslavia."
- "Ergo, Itzhak = Simon."

This is a textbook case of denial. Any well-adjusted person is able to admit that Yugoslavia no longer exists since the division of the Eastern Bloc.

SYMPTOMS

STAGE ONE: Upon deluding yourself that your new friends are just like your old friends, you assume you already know everything about them. You are disappointed when they do not behave accordingly:

". . . And then there was the time I shaved off my pubic hair and skipped naked through the quad," Simon blurts out unexpectedly one day. This shatters your image of Simon. "Itzhak would *never* have done anything as foolish as that," you lament. "Itzhak would have *galloped*."

STAGE TWO: In this phase of the illness, you become despondent upon realizing that your new friends do not fit neatly into a nice little group. You repress the fact that your old friends did not fit neatly into a nice little group either, though they did happen to spend a lot of time together. Still, in a desperate attempt to re-create the bygone gang, you invite all your new friends over to bond via brunch and Wiffle ball. This only aggravates the sickness, since no one is very nice when they have to get up early to wash dishes and strike out with a bunch of people they don't know.

STAGE THREE: The final phase is characterized by the calamitous mixing of new friends and old friends. You are convinced that both parties will get along swimmingly since they are so alike. Instead:

1. Your old friends do not like your new friends.

2. Your new friends do not like your old friends.

3. Everyone is very hostile when they meet the person they have been told is so much like themselves. Especially when his name is Itzhak.

RECOVERY

Resolving the None of My New Friends Are as Cool as My Old Friends syndrome requires a long-term treatment plan. Victims must move into a dormitory-like institution with their new friends, where they will live, fight, and emotionally abuse each other over a four-year period. Upon release, they will feel that their new friends are, indeed, just as cool as their old friends.

If this treatment proves ineffective for you, do not despair. Once you have invested the years and energy necessary to cultivate a new set of friends, they will all move away to other cities. Thus, the affliction disappears by itself.

FROM KEGGER TO COCKTAIL: PARTIES OF THE REAL WORLD

In the Real social World, it is no longer possible to wake up one morning, think to yourself, "Self, I believe I will have a party this evening," and magically have a roomful of funsters there by 9:30. Mixers, matchers, and formals will no longer be psychically willed by someone else and transmitted telepathically to you. Now if you want to have a party, you will have to take more drastic measures, such as planning it. You may even have to inform others of its occurrence. This is done with something called an invitation.[5]

TABLE 1: THE EVOLUTION OF THE INVITATION

Self, I Believe I will have a party.

[a]   *pre-evolutionary college period.*

Hello? I am going to have a party.

[b]   *early Social Lifer.*

PARTY AT MY PLACE 2-NITE B.Y.O.B. 9:00PM-9:00AM B.Y.O.B.

[c]   *tool-using Lifer.*

[5] *Pronounced:* "In-vit-ay-shun"

WHO TO INVITE

You will be pleased to discover that it's easier than ever to fill a room with partygoers. This is because your apartment is the size of Malibu Barbie and Ken's beach house, not because you have lots of friends. Luckily, you do not need many friends to have a Real-World *soirée*. What you need is for *them* to bring friends.[6] Insert a subtle reminder at the bottom of the invitation:

P.S.: PLEASE feel free to bring friends! Also, enemies/acquaintances/grandparents/pets/ those guys who live under the bridge/those girls who hang around the bus stop bathroom! Door prizes to the first fifteen people who show up with others!
Free money!

WHO NOT TO INVITE

Do not invite the neighbors. Make it clear that they are not invited by hanging an invitation on their door the day before the party. This is a Real-World signal that they should make other plans instead of banging on their walls or floor, calling the police, and screaming, *"This is not a dormitory!"* while you are trying to conduct a party.

To properly respond to an invitation hung on their door the day before the party, the neighbors will hang a thank-you note on *your* door the morning after the party. Typically, this missive begins as follows: *"This is not a dormitory!"* Be sure to save this note. It will provide guests with endless entertainment at your next party.

[e] *fully evolved Social Lifer.*

[d] *discovery of art.*

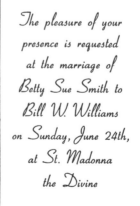

[f] *domesticated Lifer.*

---

[6] *Addendum to page 102, paragraph 2, sentence 1: It is perfectly permissible to* host *a party composed of Other People's Friends.*

PARTY POLICY: FIVE SOCIAL ORDINANCES

1. **NO SUCKING FACE.** The Real-World party is no place for public heavy petting. Do it only in the privacy of your host's bathroom.

2. **NO SINGING.** Drunken air-guitaring at parties is an embarrassing pursuit that Social Lifers cannot afford. It is more lucrative to use a real guitar at subway stations, where passengers will pay you to stop.

3. **NO TAKING OFF OF SHOES.** Unless you are hosting a Japanese tea party, never ask guests to remove footwear to keep your floor clean. Without shoes, they will feel naked. Then they won't see the need to remove the rest of their clothing.

4. **NO THEME PARTIES.** These include: costume parties; toga parties; '70s parties; summer "snowstorm" parties; winter "beach" parties; Tupperware parties; TV-based parties including Oscar, Grammy, Emmy, and Tony parties but excluding Super Bowl parties (except those that require guests to do more than eat, drink, and watch); and *especially* "come as your roommate" parties. If it is a Real-World party, your roommate will be nowhere in sight.

5. **NO SHOWING UP EMPTY-HANDED.** Give your hosts a bottle of wine. Make sure it isn't the same bottle they gave you when you had a party. If they liked that kind of wine, they would've drunk it with the people who gave it to *them* in the first place.

WHAT IF YOU ARE EVER INVITED TO A PARTY?

If you are a true Social Lifer, you will not RSVP. This is because you do not know what RSVP stands for. Fortunately, your hosts do not know what RSVP means either. If they did, they would stop asking all their guests for it and go get one themselves.

ATTENDANCE FOR CASUAL ACQUAINTANCES

If you have never met the host or are a particularly uninteresting guest, it is customary to arrive at the function exactly on time or approximately thirty minutes early. This allows you to watch your half-naked host run around frantically trying to get balloons to stick to the ceiling with static cling. Also, make sure you are the last to leave. Tack on an additional ten minutes every time your host yawns out loud and says, "Boy, am I tired." Eventually your host will get the hint and go to bed so you can finally have the place to yourself.

ATTENDANCE FOR CLOSE FRIENDS

You are under no obligation to attend the function if you are a close friend of the hosts. You know how little fun they are when they're worried that no one will attend their party. You know how anxious they get when their whole party is composed of strangers asking them, "How do you know the hosts?" Who can enjoy themselves with irritable hosts like that? Instead, get all of their other close friends together and have a party of your own.

AN ENTRY-LEVEL PARTY VARIETY-PAC

THE NEO-KEGGER In your pre-Real-Worldly years, this affair was called a "kegger," the object of which was to get so drunk that your heart began pumping Rolling Rock and your stomach began pumping blood. This behavior is no longer fashionable. It is also no longer possible. At the Neo-Kegger, even Social Lifers who *are* able to drink as much as they could in the old days are unable to become as inebriated. While no one can explain the decline of this side effect, it seems to accompany a marked rise of the morning-after effect.

The Neo-Kegger differs from its precursor in several other ways:

1. *The emergence of the Pre-Dance State.* This period follows the removal of living room furniture and precedes the onset of rhythmic motion. It is characterized by several people talking to each other in the middle of the room while swaying, snapping, tapping, and glancing at the stereo speakers. These people are also trying to ignore the scary girl who has been participating in a dance-a-thon with herself for the past three hours.

2. *The selection of the kitchen as the preferred gathering spot.* Even if the keg has been placed in the bathroom or bedroom, real Social Lifers always wind up in the kitchen by party's end. This is because they are trying to steal food.

3. *The discovery of leftover beer.* The most shocking and disturbing distinction of the Neo-Kegger.

THE COCKTAIL PARTY Eventually, drinking warm foam out of a spout connected to a garbage can may lose a certain degree of luster. It is then that you will start attending cocktail parties. The idea of a cocktail party is to accomplish with a quick couple of drinks what used to take half a keg to achieve.

When requesting a cocktail, be as specific as possible:

Don't say: *"I would like a sloe gin fizz, please."*

Do say: *"Gin, Gilbey's, slow, fizzy, straight up and on the rocks, neat, with a twist, in a frosted martini glass with a blue stripe on it and a little umbrella, no salt, with a swizzle stick—plastic, seventeen centimeters in length—and a splash. Make that a double."*

It does not matter that this drink is no longer a sloe gin fizz. Why would you want one of those anyway? They taste like expectorant. And if that is what you're craving, you should be at home in bed, not at a cocktail party.

Additionally, remember that it is no longer appropriate to drink directly out of the bottle. That is what baseball helmets with built-in straws are for. It is also no longer appropriate to mix a bottle of grape Snapple with a half-gallon of vodka and pass out on your host's floor. To get through a Real-World cocktail party, you'll want to skip the Snapple and pass out on your host's futon.

BRUNCH Brunch is the kind of party you have when you don't know enough people to have a *real* party. It is one of the most popular kinds of parties. To make brunch, you need these ingredients:

1. champagne or vodka
2. orange or tomato juice

These ingredients should be provided by your guests to thank you for making them brunch.

When going to a *restaurant* where brunch is poured, never be so crass as to bring *The New York Times* with you. Would you ever do this when going to a restaurant for dinner? Of course not—because *The New York Times* does not carry "Walter Scott's Personality Parade."

HOW TO HAVE A DINNER PARTY

The standard Real-World dinner party is the opposite of the standard Real-World dinner. Instead of making too much spaghetti, you make too little. This is no problem if there are enough chips and salsa to fill up on, which there are not. That is no problem if there is enough garlic bread to fill up on, which there is, though it's on fire. That is no problem since there will be enough Ben & Jerry's to fill up on later, as long as your guests brought straws. If they didn't, tell them to dip the remaining chips into it and pretend it is the salsa. That will be no problem if they have filled up on enough E-Z TwistOff red wine, which they most definitely have. After all, they've been waiting for something to eat for several hours.

When hosting a Real-World dinner party, be as distinctive with the table setting as you are with the food. Fortunately, there is nothing as distinctive as the plastic *Make Way for Duck-*

Pop Quiz

ARE YOU LIVING IN THE REAL WORLD?

1. Do you own a mop?
2. Is there a stick of butter in your refrigerator butter tray?
3. Do you secretly read wedding announcements in the newspaper?
4. When paying bills, are you careful to write your account number on the check?
5. Does your fan "oscillate"?

lings plate you got when you began teething, a knife you stole from the college cafeteria, a fork you stole from Roy Rogers', the Chewbacca glass you got the night *Star Wars* opened, and a wood-veneer salad bowl of unknown origin. Do not worry about getting such fine china dirty. Your company will wash all the dishes after dinner. To be polite, you should say: "Why, that is not necessary. You are the *guests*." Mutter this under your breath in a barely audible tone and immediately depart the kitchen.

When attending a Real-World dinner party, remember: You are the *guest*. Instead of washing all the dishes after dinner, simply pretend to start washing one of them. Listen carefully for the words, "Why, that is not necessary." To be polite, stop washing and immediately depart the kitchen.

There are several equally appetizing variations of the standard Real-World dinner party:

THE BARBECUE The point of a barbecue is to hover over a blistering grill until your own sweat marinates the meat. This grill should be the one the last tenants left behind, with years' worth of encrusted carcinogens to add zest to any entrée. Or, if you prefer serving blackened hands for dinner, purchase a collapsible barbecue guaranteed to collapse whenever you flip a burger. As you engage in self-immolation, your guests should be off playing volleyball, zipping across a slip-and-slide, or performing other barbecue-oriented recreation, such as torturing the neighbor's cat. Dinner is served when the delectable aroma of lighter fluid has wafted through the apartment building, fumigating to death at least one occupant. **DRESS CODE:** *flame-retardant.* **ESSENTIAL GUEST:** *strict vegetarian.* **BYO:** *oxygen mask.*

THE POTLUCK There is nothing Real-World about a dinner party where you are required to bring the dinner. That is why you should never go to potlucks. You should only host them.

The potluck is so named because, with luck, someone will bring pot. Smoked as an *hors d'oeuvre*, this dish will whet your guests' appetites to the point that they will devour even the Tuna Noodle-O's Helper, marsh-mallow Spam surprise, and Chef Boyardee they brought to your dinner party. **DRESS CODE:** *hemp.* **ESSENTIAL GUEST:** *Birkenstock-clad member of food co-op.* **BYO:** *hors d'oeuvres.*

THE HIGH-RENT CATERED AFFAIR As you climb ahead in the Real social World, you will make certain friends who invite you over for a little something they've "whipped up" and then serve you a banquet on matching plates that do not rip when they get wet. A favorite dish is free-range sun-dried goat cheese vinaigrette with warm raspberry cilantro radicchio focaccia risotto on a couscous bed of arugula pesto. With pine nuts. To cleanse the palate, they provide an expensive, chilled chianti '78 cabernet beaujolais zinfandel pinot grigio sauvignon, served in wine glasses, not Dixie riddle cups. For dessert, there are berries. And cappuccino.

Eating at these people's dinner parties is like eating at a fancy restaurant. This makes sense, since that is where the food really came from. The only difference is that now you are made to feel inadequate by a close friend, not a surly waiter. **DRESS CODE:** *dinner jacket.* **ESSENTIAL GUEST:** *pretentious art history Ph.D. candidate.* **BYO:** *Ring-Dings.*

THE LOW-RENT CATERED AFFAIR As you lag behind in the Real social World, you will make certain friends you invite over for a little something you've "whipped up" and then serve a banquet you've removed from buckets that rip when they get wet. A favorite dish is Kentucky fried extra crispy hot 'n' spicy, three drumsticks, five wings, four breasts, two thighs with one jumbo cole slaw, a side of potato salad, and a large fries. With biscuits. To cleanse the palate, you provide a cheap, warm Budweiser 6 served in cans, not bottles. For dessert, there are Ring-Dings. And Yoo-Hoo.

Eating at your dinner party is like eating at a fast-food restaurant. This makes sense, since that is where the food really came from. The only difference is that now your friends are made to feel nauseated in your home, not theirs. **DRESS CODE:** *T-shirt with dinner jacket painted on.* **ESSENTIAL GUEST:** *starving artist.* **BYO:** *Beano.*

Pop Quiz

ARE YOU LIVING IN THE REAL WORLD?

1. Do you own four or more dishes that match?

2. Have you ever purchased "travel-size" toiletries?

3. Do you "tidy up" before friends come over?

4. Is there a movie schedule from some funky theater hanging on your refrigerator?

5. Do you know where your college diploma is?

ENTRY-LEVEL RECREATION

No matter where you recreate in the Real World, you will hear Social Lifers saying the same things:

a. "There is nothing to do here."

b. "There is a lot to do here, and I cannot afford any of it."

c. "I'll wait until it comes out on video."

Therefore, what you do for fun in the Real World is not all that different from what you did for fun in college: drinking, eating, and drug abuse. It's simply the *approach* that differs.

GOING OUT FOR "ADRINK"

In your pre-Real-World years, you went out drinking. Now you will go out for "adrink." You will go out for "adrink" because you have to wake up for "aJob," and attendance counts.

Sadly, some Social Lifers deal with this demanding schedule by abstaining from alcohol. Worse, they start drinking to the point of moderation. They replace jumbo pitchers of beer with a singular "adrink" of their own, such as scotch and water. Or water and water. Or lime Gatorade, which they take straight up at the juice bar in their gym.

As a self-respecting Social Lifer, do not succumb to such peer pressure. Each weeknight, appoint yourself the "designated adrinker." Plan to meet several "adrinking buddies" at various locations throughout the evening. By having one stiff "adrink" with each, you'll get just as sloppy as you did yesteryear, but in a far more responsible manner.

REAL-WORLD DRINKING GAMES

When the weekend rolls around, it's back to your devil-may-care ways. To unwind and reduce stress, there's nothing healthier than some alcohol-based fun and games:

QUARTERS

1. Bring quarters to laundromat.
2. Discover no available machines.
3. Use quarters to buy beer.

HIGH BILL

Based on the classic college drinking game "Hi Bob," in which players watch the old *Bob Newhart Show* and imbibe whenever characters say, "Hi, Bob." In the Real-World version, players do not watch *Newhart*, since the cable company has disconnected their service. Instead, they drink whenever they get a high electric, gas, or credit card bill. Whoever gets liver cirrhosis first wins.

PATHETIC, MAUDLIN OLD DRUNK

Played alone with a fifth of scotch and a stack of photos from sophomore spring break.

RECREATIONAL EATING

Before long, a "party" will come to mean the number of people you are with at a restaurant. Thanks to your whopping new salary, the days of "dining and dashing" are over. They have been replaced by the days of "chewing and charging." If the restaurant does not take credit cards,[7] take a quick dash down memory lane.

When dining at restaurants with less accessible exits, always bring a notepad and pen. Scribble disapprovingly after each bite of your burrito. Ask the manager detailed questions, such as: "Is the *foie gras* at this establishment French imported or domestic?" Soon he or she will suspect that you are a restaurant critic. To confirm these suspicions, act professional: Say you will pan the restaurant unless you get free food.

---

[7] *that are completely overdrawn*

How to Select the Wine
Begin by perusing the wine list as if you can either pronounce or afford any of the selections. If you are having red meat, the proper wine to order is known as "house red." If you are having poultry, a delightful little vintage called "house white" is the wine for you. Always accept the waitperson's offer to sample the wine. Take a whiff, swish it around your mouth like Listerine, gargle, and spit it out on the waitperson's apron in disgust. Next, angrily state the following: "You call *this* house white? Preposterous!" Nine times out of ten you will get a free bottle.

THE SOCIAL FOOD CHAIN: SURVIVAL OF THE FATTEST

As leisure time dwindles in the Real social World, friends fall into place on the social food chain: lunch friends, brunch friends, and those nearly extinct social organisms, dinner dates. Such habitats evolve in a Darwinian manner. Lunch friends may eventually be digested into real friends, while real friends are often chewed up and spit out as brunch friends. The guide below will help you establish an effective pecking order:

LUNCH FRIENDS: *[a]* friends you call up and identify yourself to by both first and last names because you still don't think they'll remember who you are, *[b]* friends with expense accounts, *[c]* friends with job contacts

BRUNCH FRIENDS: anyone you got drunk with the night before

HAPPY HOUR FRIENDS: *[a]* friends who are bartenders, *[b]* other people's friends who are bartenders

COFFEE FRIENDS: friends you see only when your therapist is on Martha's Vineyard

BREAKFAST FRIENDS: the girl who works at McDonald's

DINNER FRIENDS: *[a]* friends you go out with: Dad, Mom, *[b]* friends you have over: anyone who ever helped you move; couple friends; the pizza delivery guy, *[c]* friends who have you over: friends who work in soup kitchens

DINNER DATES: see "imaginary friends," p. 103

MULTICULTURAL EATING

The Real-World palate is one that appreciates culinary delicacies from nations far and wide. It is also one that cannot afford to visit these nations. Such is the beauty of ethnic restaurants. Eating at these establishments provides all the adventure and derring-do of junior year abroad.[8] Therefore, approach them in the same manner: Act as American as possible. Before you order, consult the following chart:

ETHNIC RESTAURANT	WHAT TO ORDER THAT RESEMBLES SOMETHING AMERICAN	WHAT IT RESEMBLES
Middle Eastern	hummus	Lipton onion-soup dip mix
Spanish	huevos rancheros	eggs and Fritos
Thai	chicken or beef saté	shish kebab with peanut butter
Chinese	cold sesame noodles	cold spaghetti with peanut butter
Indian	poori with chutney	peanut butter and jelly sandwich without peanut butter
Japanese	tempura	Shake 'n Bake
Mexican	chicken molé	chicken with hot fudge sauce
Ethiopian	anything	Cycle Three dog food

[8] *including the intestinal parasites*

YOUR CHANGING SUBSTANCE ABUSE PATTERNS

Doping oneself up with powerful narcotics is an excellent way to enjoy one's stay in the Real World. This task requires a more serious commitment than before, however. In college, you could always count on that guy with the Tai Chi pants and the beeper to show up at every party with free samples of his latest harvest. That guy isn't around anymore. He is now working on Wall Street.

Yet it is not necessary to travel all the way to Wall Street to get drugs.[9] If you are willing to experiment, a whole new pharmacopoeia awaits you from a number of convenient connections:

DRUGS OF THE REAL WORLD

NYQUIL: One shot of this firewater before bed and your mellow won't be harshed when your roommate decides to watch *Earthquake* in sense-O-round at three o'clock in the morning. **STREET NAME:** snooze booze. **WHERE TO SCORE:** aisle 5B at Walgreen's, across from "hair color"

XANAX: The XTC of the Real World. From anxiety dreams about work to anxiety nightmares *at* work, these prescription poppers depress all the right panic buttons. **STREET NAME:** brain enema. **WHERE TO SCORE:** new best friend[10]; mother's purse

SMART DRUGS: These placebos cause hallucinations of intelligence in users stupid enough to believe they work. For a tastier buzz, inhale a bag of SmartFood and pop a fistful of Smarties. **STREET NAME:** dumb drugs. **WHERE TO SCORE:** genius at a rave

DEXATRIM: Wash these uppers back with an office-coffee chaser for a speedball to keep you collating right through your lunch break. **STREET NAME:** dieter's delight. **WHERE TO SCORE:** friend with eating disorder

THERAFLU: A mug of hot water laced with this uncut white powder brings you down to a lightheaded, heavylidded groove. **STREET NAME:** electric Kool-Aid. **WHERE TO SCORE:** dishonest cocaine dealer

ROBITUSSIN MAXIMUM STRENGTH COUGH SYRUP: Trip out on mind-expanding dextromethorphan for a psychedelic sensation with a pleasant cherry flavor. **STREET NAME:** liquid sunshine. **WHERE TO SCORE:** Kitty Dukakis

VICKS VAPORUB: Take a hit off these fumes when you're jonesin' for a fast headrush, or rub it all over for a full-contact high. **STREET NAME:** Vicky V. **WHERE TO SCORE:** grandfather's medicine cabinet

UNREAL-WORLDLY RECREATION

The sophisticated Social Lifer will outgrow the following in no more than three years:

-animation festival

-sports bar

-Renaissance fair

-moshing

-waterfront eating and shopping emporiums

-beverages with such names as "Fuzzy Navel" and "Sex on the Beach"

-Hard Rock Café

-Padre Island, TX

-Daytona Beach, FL

-Virginia Beach, VA

-booze cruise

-George Winston

-laser show

-clove cigarettes

-beverages served in bowls

-beer bong

1ST IN A SERIES: Real-Worldly Things to Do When You Are Not Eating, Drinking, or Doing Drugs (and Even When You Are)

VISIT A MUSEUM!
When visiting a museum, rent a pair of headsets to hear a recorded walking tour of the exhibit. Bring your own tapes to stay awake until you get to the gift shop.

[9] *unless you want the really good stuff*
[10] *see "New Best Friends," page 103*

The Little Chill

Once you've been in the Real social World a few years, you'll want to drop back in on your old college gang. The fact that your old college gang is now scattered across the Western Hemisphere is inconsequential. With the help of your long-distance WATS line at work, it's easy to round up those lifelong chums: **YOU:** "Scooter! How *are* you? It's *Babs*!"
LIFELONG CHUM: "Who?"

After abducting the old gang, regress to the pre-Real-World state. Drink vast amounts of beer, wine, vanilla extract, witch hazel, etc. Dance naked on the table tops. It doesn't matter that you never did these things in college. What matters is that you *pretend* you did, so you can pretend you're having just as much fun now as you did then. Especially the dry-heaving part.

Behaving in this manner will also help you adjust to your changing chums. In all likelihood, your chum who used to have a fuchsia mohawk will now be a vice-president at Merrill Lynch. Your chum who used to be chairperson of Campus Born Agains will now be chairperson of Queer Nation. You will now be a respectable, ambitious graduate with a promising future. For the quintessential gathering, it is also imperative to adhere to these rules:

- One chum must bring an uninvited girlfriend or boyfriend everyone pretends not to hate.
- Two chums who were "just friends" in college must now be engaged.
- One chum must be going bald.
- One chum must be a Scientologist.

If conversation seems strained now that you all have nothing in common, why dwell upon the present? Instead, recount that wild party freshman year when Babs threw the cat out the window to see if it would land on all fours. Move on to that wild party sophomore year when you all got to ride in the fire engine. And what about that *wild* party junior year when Becky gave birth? Not to mention that *profoundly* wild party senior year when you all threw *yourselves* out the window because you thought you were the Superfriends. Analyze each of these incidents from twenty-seven different angles, exploring every conceivable point of view. Repeat.

When everyone is convinced that he or she had a terrific time in college, convince each other that you are having a terrific time in the Real World. Your chum who hates living in Montana because he has no friends should say: "I love living in Montana because I have a special relationship with nature!" Your chum who is an unemployed actor moonlighting as a birthday-party clown should say: "I am a performance artist with many adoring young fans!" You should say: "My apartment does not have plywood boards nailed to the windows! My boss is not violently insane! I have gone on many fabulous dates!"

The reunion concludes when the sun comes up, just like the old days. But now, each chum must turn to each other chum and say: "Good morning! I did not fall asleep at ten-thirty p.m.!"

REAL-WORLD DATING TIPS

HOW TO BREAK UP

The first thing you must do to meet that special Entry-Level someone is dispose of your college girlfriend, boyfriend, both, whatever. Now that your irises have adjusted to the bright sunlight, you can see that these people are not for you. If they were, you would be living where they are, they would be living where you are, or you would both be living in San Francisco. If you already find yourself in one of these places, do not worry. You can still break up. Use any of the following "code" lines to make it perfectly clear that it's all over:

1. "I'll give you a call."
2. "I had a good time."
3. "Can I have that ten bucks you owe me?"

Remember, breaking up can be a painful, lonely experience. To avoid getting hurt, stay with your current mate while you search for someone better.[11]

STARTING OVER

There are many advantages to Real-World dating. Unlike in college, the male/female ratio is the same. If you are male, the ratio of men to women is 1:0, and if you are female, the ratio of women to men is 1:0.

Another advantage of Real-World dating is that everyone you'll be going out with has recently been "hurt." Chances are, you'll remind them of the person they have been "hurt" by. See, you already have something in common! If you have not been "hurt," act as though you have. Say, "I am feeling very vulnerable right now," or, "I have finally learned to enjoy my freedom." As long as you act like someone who does not want to date, you will get many dates.

It may also be worth noting that anyone you meet in the Real World could be the person with whom you will spend the rest of your life (see below).

A GUIDE TO LOWERING YOUR STANDARDS

Finding someone to spend the rest of your life with is different from finding someone to go to the semiformal with. For one thing, the dress code is not as clear. For another, you will be expected to remember the person's name when you wake up with him or her in the morning. This type of pressure causes many Social Lifers to form unreasonable expectations. In their search for the ideal mate, they expect to find someone with not only the right clothes, but also a memorable name. Rest assured; Mr. or Ms. Right *is* out there. But before you find him or her, you have to adjust your standards:

UNREAL-WORLD STANDARD	REAL-WORLD STANDARD
You want someone intelligent.	You want someone who does not sound out words while reading.
You want someone with a sense of humor.	You want someone who is not addicted to Prozac.
You want a man who looks like Keanu Reeves.	You want a man who does not look like the late Hervé Villechaize.
You want a woman who looks like Naomi Campbell.	You want a woman who does not look like Weezie from *The Jeffersons*.
You want someone who is mature.	You want someone who can ride a two-wheeler.
You want someone with a nice body.	You want someone who can see his or her feet.
You want someone with wavy hair and pouty lips.	You want someone without a harelip.
You believe in love at first sight.	You believe everyone looks better after a few drinks.

2ND IN A SERIES: Real-World Things to Do When You Are Not Eating, Drinking, or Doing Drugs (and Even When You Are)

GO TO A COMEDY CLUB! *In the Real social World, everybody is a comedian. And they are all performing at comedy clubs. This is because they are not funny enough to get their own TV show. If a good laugh is what you're after, go to a poetry reading.*

[11] *better-looking, better off, better apartment, better car, better in bed, etc.*

LOOKING FOR MR. OR MS. OKAY

Once you've formed an image of your perfect partner, obtain her or him. The search is far more exciting now that you're not limited to the thousands of potential dates who surrounded you every day in the dorm, in classes, at parties, in the library, in the cafeteria, at the pub, at the game, in the student union, at the bookstore, in your room, in your bed, etc. In the Real World, there's mystery; there's intrigue. Anyone you date could turn out to be that machete-wielding crackhead of your dreams.

If you expect to find your ideal mate, you've got to get into circulation and start looking. But, as your smarmy "couple friends" are happy to point out, you're not going to find anyone until you stop looking. The obvious solution is to get out into circulation and start looking but ignore anyone who seems like your ideal mate.

GETTING FIXED UP

To lessen the chances of meeting your ideal mate, get set up through mutual friends. How about your friend's sister? Your sister's friend? Your friend's brother? Your own brother? If you do not have siblings, try your friend's friend; a friend of a friend of a friend; someone you picked up at Radio Shack. What all of these people have in common is that they are complete and total strangers.[12] You might be able to convince one of them to go out with you.

It can be tricky to get fixed up through a friend, especially because your friend is usually dating the person you really want. Do not jeopardize your friendship by becoming a tawdry homewrecker. Instead, politely *ask* to be set up with your friend's mate. If this is a good friend, he or she will happily oblige. If not, this person was never really your friend in the first place, and you may commence with homewrecking.

THE PERSONAL ADS

Place a personal ad to assist in the process of elimination. Eliminate anyone who responds.

These people are looking for the kind of person you are not. They are looking for the kind of person you described in your personal ad. And if they are that gullible, you're better off without them.

For example, say you are writing a personal ad and you possess the following virtues:

You are a **twelve-foot albino beast** with an **extra arm** and a **plate in your head**. Friends say you resemble the **Elephant Man**. You are looking for a **hideous midget speed freak** with **no eyes**.

To weed out the losers, word your ad as follows:

> I am **tall**, **Nordic**, and **rugged**; a **great hugger** with a **solid head on my shoulders**. Friends say I resemble **Superman**. You are **unconventional**, **petite**, **active**, and will **see** me for who I really am. Respond now.

Obviously, anyone who responds to this ad is not going to be your type, and you are not going to be theirs. In one simple step, you've pared down your search to the cream of the crop.

TRUE OFFICE ROMANCE

You gaze at her collating by the Xerox machine and it is all you can do to contain your throbbing manhood. You stare at him tabulating a printout of vendor satisfaction surveys and you become weak with desire. You've both tried to fight these primal urges, yet finally you surrender. Soon you are rolling naked around the supply room floor, body-painting each other with Wite-Out.

If this scene sounds familiar, you are treading on dangerous ground. Wite-Out, after all, contains potentially toxic fumes.

Remember: the key to a successful office affair is keeping it secret. That way, you can kid yourself into believing that everyone from the janitor on up doesn't already know. For example, if the two of you have a horrible fight one night, make sure you slam a lot of doors and scream at each other at work the next day. By acting like everyone else, you'll ensure that no one will suspect a thing.

[12] *especially your brother*

Additionally, be sure to get involved with an associate who is both powerful and married. In the best-case scenario, you will score yourself a bigger cube without having to make any messy long-term commitments. Avoid anyone who seems even slightly appropriate. In the worst-case scenario, you will score yourself a lifelong companion and become one of those tedious couples who talk only about work.

MEAT MARKETS AND SINGLES BARS

There is no place better than a crowded meat market to pick up a randy Social Lifer. Slide up to the deli counter, tell the butcher you want a quarter pound of the rump—lean—and you never know who you'll be sharing your cold cuts with later in the evening. Of course, the delicatessen is just one of many *très chic* meeting spots for today's safe-sex swinger. If *you* are on the make for a disease-free sweetheart, you will also want to check out the chart below.

THE DATE PART

After using the aforementioned techniques to find the person with whom you'll spend the rest of your life, go out on a date first, just to be sure. Here are several dating options:

BLIND DATES

The formula for a successful blind date is:

Drinks/Movie/Dessert/Settle Down and Start a Family

PHASE ONE: Drinks. Drinks should take place in a well-lit public arena no more than one half hour before the movie. This allows adequate time to escape if your date appears to be (a) covered with boils from head to toe, or (b) capable of dismembering you later in the evening.

3RD IN A SERIES: Real-Worldly Things to Do When You Are Not Eating, Drinking, or Doing Drugs (and Even When You Are)

ATTEND A CONCERT! Rowdy rock clubs were fine in your pre-Real-World years, but now you must expand your musical tastes to include jazz; classical; opera. By hobnobbing with patrons of the arts, you can scalp your tickets for far more money. And you won't have to spend a week scrubbing an ink stamp off your hand.

SINGLES BARS OF THE REAL WORLD

REAL-WORLD SINGLES BAR	WHERE THE ACTION IS	PICKUP LINE
Grocery Store	Produce Aisle	"Excuse me, you look like someone who knows how to tell if a cantaloupe is ripe . . ."
Health Club	Bench Press	"I hear the bun-burners class is quite a workout!"
Laundromat	Folding Table	"I bet you look great in those."
Adult Education Center	Wine-Tasting Class	"I'm so wasted. Wanna go back to my place?"
12-Step Program	A.A.	"I'm so sober. Wanna go back to my place?"
Video Store	"Adult" Section	"I like to watch."
Bookstore	Womyn's Studies	"Didn't I see you at the Clog-A-Thon for Empowerment last night?"
Public Transportation	Night Train	"Have You Ever Seen *Risky Business*?"
Professional Organization	Real Estate	"Let's go screw people."
Wedding	Open Bar[13]	"Will you marry me?"

[13] *For Jewish weddings, substitute Dessert Smorgasbord.*

PHASE TWO: Movie. The purpose of the movie is threefold:

1. It gives you something to talk about during phase one (drinks).
2. It gives you something to do so you don't have to talk to each other during phase two (movie).
3. It gives you something to talk about during phase three (dessert).

PHASE THREE: Dessert. Dessert is a chance to discuss the movie. How did you like it? How did your date like it? Based on this discussion, you will be able to tell if you would like to settle down with this person and start a family.

PHASE FOUR: Settle Down and Start a Family. Same as above but with stronger drinks, the Nickelodeon Network, and a fat-free birthday cake from Entenmann's.

TIME-SAVING DATES

The idea here is to minimize time wasted in the search for Mr. or Ms. Okay. The next time you meet a subject with whom you wish to spend the rest of your life, do not go on a date with him or her. Instead, go on a date with his or her father or mother. That way, you'll know immediately what sort of nut the subject will turn out to be should you decide to spend the rest of your lives together.

If you hit it off with Mom or Dad, arrange a second date with their offspring. Spend this date traveling for a week together in a car.[14] If one of you does not bring intentional early death upon the other by date's end, consider yourselves compatible and proceed to spend the rest of your lives together.

DREAM DATES

These most often take the form of recurring nightmares that have you clutching the sheets and crying out, "Mommy!" Expect to experience one or all of the following disturbing motifs:

THE FRESHMAN FLASHBACK. The rendezvous gets under way at O.G. Willikins Saloon and Eating Emporium: Good Friends, Good Times! Lies, both. It is Jell-O–shot Happy Hour and you are the only Emporium-goer who is legal. To complement the Jell-O, your date orders melted cheese–covered potato skins, melted cheese–covered buffalo wings, and melted cheese–covered fried cheese sticks. You order several gelatin-free chasers to wash it all back. Soon you become bombed. You know this because you are starting to have fun. "Let's motor-vate down to the Arm Pit," your date suggests. "There's this *totally* dope band there that sounds *totally* like Pearl Jam 'cept they only do Doors covers." "Totally," you say, barely. You get to the Arm Pit. Judging by the aroma, it is appropriately named. So is the band. They are called Door Jam. You fight your way to the bar and order two shots of Cuervo—one for you, and the other for . . . you. Soon you become ill. "I have become ill," you tell your date. "Totally," comes the response. The next afternoon, you wake up with a migraine and an unsightly stranger. You fear there is a connection.

THE CULTURE CRASH. You have long stopped pretending that you'd rather do something sophisticated and cultural than stay home and watch *The Bradys' 89th Reunion: Alice Finally Dies,* but the fact remains: You've already seen that one. You start things off at your companion's "favorite little South Papua New Guinean trattoria," where you are served something that looks like roadkill. You excuse yourself to go to the bathroom, which happens to be at the Jack in the Box across the street. Soon you find yourself at one of the following rest spots: symphony, ballet, opera, subtitled film, *Hamlet.* Throughout, your date whispers sweet nothings into your ear, such as: "The final denouement in act two hints of the tragic yet Faustian hubris so typical of the early classicists." You rack your brain for the perfect reply. "Did you ever see the one where they go to Hawaii and meet Vincent Price?" you say.

THE OUTWARD BOUND. "Don't forget to bend your knees!" your date calls out as you are

Pop Quiz

ARE YOU LIVING IN THE REAL WORLD?

1. Do you take vitamins?
2. Do you separate your whites from your colors?
3. Do you have a photo of a loved one on your desk at work?
4. Have you ever voluntarily eaten a "turkey burger"?
5. Do you own a soup ladle?

14 *un-air-conditioned*

about to bungee-jump off a bridge to your death below. You wonder how you ever got yourself into this position. You do not even *like* the outdoors. It seemed so innocent at first—that afternoon bike ride, that mixed doubles match where you were allowed to hit the ball on the third bounce. One thing led to another and soon you found yourself cross-country skiing; jogging; wearing hiking boots to dinner parties. But now, you realize all of this is heading for only one thing: the camping trip. You have always been a firm believer that camping trips are best reserved for deranged retirees in RVs with bumper stickers that say, "Ask me about my grandchildren!" It finally dawns on you: You haven't been dating, you've been training. If you wanted a trainer, you'd go to the gym. You remove your bungee cords. You go to the gym. You head for the sauna, light up a butt, and hope to meet someone more your type.

THE SOLILOQUY. You are on a date and you are engaged in the following conversation:

YOU:

DATE: ". . . and then I graduated and then I moved to Idaho because I didn't think I could survive Iowa and then I got an ideal job at IHOP and then I backpacked around Ireland and I read the *I Ching* and then I knew what I wanted to do was I wanted to help people so I had this idea that I could try to help the blind by breeding seeing-eye dogs and that's what led me to apply to IU to get my M.E. and I realized Grandma Ina was right when she told me I could do anything I wanted when I was just knee-high with poison ivy and I really wanted to play the Popeye song "I Am What I Am and That's What I Am" in the first grade piano recital so what I did was I practiced and I practiced and I . . ."

THE DISASTROUS DINNER. You are trapped in an empty Italian restaurant with someone who looks and acts nothing like you remember from the party where you first met. Your date has forced you to change tables three times. It was too drafty, too stuffy, and too close to the bathroom. It is like going out with your parents. You are eating ziti. The cheese is dripping all over your chin. Your date is not eating dinner. It is being recooked. It was "raw." Then it was "charred." You tell a story about your evil boss. Your date turns out to be her cousin. You tell a little joke. Your date says, "Did that really happen?" The check comes. Your date tells the waitress she is not getting a tip. The waitress rips off her apron and storms out of the restaurant, tears streaming down her cheeks. You offer to pay the check. Your date says no, you should split it. You agree. Your date says you owe eighty-six cents more because you asked for the parmesan cheese and they charge extra for that.

MORE DREAM DATES

THE HOMOSEXUAL ENCOUNTER. You are on a date with someone who has been eyeing members of the same sex all night.

THE HETEROSEXUAL ENCOUNTER. You are on a date with someone who has been eyeing members of the opposite sex all night.

THE BESTIALITY ENCOUNTER. You are on a date with someone who has been eyeing members of opposite species all night.

THE MASOCHISTIC ENCOUNTER. You are on a date with someone your parents fixed you up with.

THE SUICIDAL ENCOUNTER. You are on a date with someone you went to the senior prom with.

THE TRICK. You are on a date with someone who asks you to put $20 at the foot of the bed before having sex.

THE REBOUND. You are on a date with someone who talks all night about a ten-year love affair that ended this morning.

THE SYMPATHY CALL. You are on a date with someone you dislike but feel sorry for.

THE CRYING GAME. You are on a date with someone who is not telling you something very important.

SEX IN THE REAL WORLD

There are many striking differences between Real-World sex and Unreal-World sex, chief among which is that your college roommate will no longer be in the room during the act itself.[15] Additionally, you will know you have progressed to Real-World sex if you have incorporated any of the following elements into your lovemaking routine:

1. a partner
2. wordless "ambient" music
3. massage oil you have purchased from The Body Shop
4. contraception you have not purchased from the restroom vending machine
5. an additional fifty-seven minutes
6. a set of clothes for the next day

TALKING DIRTY

Ultimately, the difference between Real-World sex and Unreal-World sex can be boiled down to this: In the Real World, people *talk* during sex. Here are some of the things they say:

"No, a little lower—yes, there. Higher. A bit more to the right, no, one and a quarter millimeters to the left. Can you turn the music down three notches? A little faster. Slower. Harder. Softer. There. Here . . ."

In other words, Real-World copulators know exactly what they want.

A. WHAT REAL-WORLD MEN WANT
Oral Stimulation

B. WHAT REAL-WORLD WOMEN WANT
Oral Stimulation

C. WHAT THE DIFFERENCE IS
In the Real World, it is no longer permissible to ignore statement B.

For further reading on sexual matters, consult the medical reference guides: *Are You*
There, God? It's Me, Margaret; Then Again, Maybe I Won't; and *Forever.* Copulators requiring special back support equipment may refer to *Deenie.*

FROM ONE-NIGHTERS TO ALL-LIFERS

In your pre-Real-World years, it was all too easy to assume that every Jane or John you picked up at a tailgate party was a nice, innocent student[16] from the suburbs. Now that you're a single parent with a festering open sore on your genitalia, you realize your youthful naïveté. It is the age of monogamy. One-night stands are deadly, irresponsible, and immature. One-night stands are empty and adolescent. In the Real World, there is no such thing as a one-night stand.

When engaging in a one-night stand, there are three things you must now do: (1) Use protection (2) Feel guilty (3) Begin a "Relationship." If the idea of a "Relationship" scares you, just think of it as a series of well-protected, guilt-free, one-night stands.

HOW TO PROPOSE

Before consummating a "Relationship," it is also vital to pop the question. Yet bashful Social Lifers often find it difficult to come right out and ask, *"Have you been tested?"* If you are ready to take that plunge and exchange the sacred bodily fluids, there are many more romantic ways to pop the question:

• *"So, ever shared a needle with a heroin addict?"*

• *"I hear Haiti is very nice this time of year."*

• *"Bisexuality certainly seems to be all the rage these days, huh?"*

• *"How do you think it would feel to be a hemophiliac?"*

[15] *when not invited*

[16] *or professor*

ENTRY-LEVEL EROTIC AIDS

As you leave behind the sheltered sexuality of your college years, you'll find yourself becoming more adventurous and daring. Who knows? You might even have sex. To expand your sexual horizons, deflate your current lover and start experimenting with a whole new range of *Real* sex toys. The sampling described here can help fulfill every Social Lifer's wildest erotic fantasies: prevention of death, disease, and, in many cases, even children.

SEX TOY	TURN-ONS	TURN-OFFS
Dental Dam	Recommended by 4 out of 5 dentists surveyed	Not covered by most dental plans
The Sponge	Combined with contraceptive foam, can be used to clean bathroom after sex	Combined with contraceptive foam, can make sex as appealing as cleaning bathroom
Male Condom	*Latex:* available free in grammar schools *Lambskin:* almost as good as sex with lambs	Packaged in user-proof armored foil
Female Condom	Doubles as Hefty bag	Engineering degree prerequisite
The Pill	Comes with handsome green or orange carrying case/calendar	Male users report better results with vasectomy
Contraceptive Jelly	More effective than grape jelly, jam, or preserves	Unpleasant chemical aftertaste when eaten with peanut butter
Norplant Implants	Safer than silicone implants	Difference in breast size is often undetectable
Foaming Suppository	Provides grownup alternative to Pop Rocks	It's a *suppository*
Diaphragm	Prolongs foreplay	Foreplay is conducted alone, in a bathroom, until sex toy is in place
Abstinence	Underwear ads in Sunday newspaper supplement	Cold showers

SECTION

VI

Entry-Level Epilogue

SURVIVING YOUR

THE FOUR-YEAR ITCH:

After about four years in the Real World, you may begin feeling somewhat restless, or somewhat prone to putting a gun to your head to relieve the crippling monotony. This is perfectly healthy.[1] After all, you've lived your life in four-year increments up until now, graduating or being

MID-MIDLIFE CRISIS

expelled into the next rousing phase of your voyage from freshman to senior. Now that you're in the Real World, however, you may look around after four years and wonder what you have to show for yourself. An apartment? *You bet!* A job? *Absolutely!* A social life? . . . An apartment? *You bet!*

In other words, you have achieved—basically—all you set out to achieve. But still, you're dispirited. "It all seems so p-p-*permanent*," you lament, detecting a strange new speech impediment. "What's the *next* big, new adventure I will have?"

Relax. If these feelings persist, you are going to have a very big, very new adventure indeed! It is called a Mid-Midlife Crisis.

DANGER SIGNS OF THE MID-MIDLIFE CRISIS

—You are an investment banker who suddenly wants to pursue a "socially responsible career."

—You are a social worker who suddenly wants to pursue a "paying career."

—You start paying attention to the ads in back of *Rolling Stone* for "High-Paying Fish-Cannery Jobs In Alaska!"

[1] *unless the gun is not a Super Soaker*

1. Which do you prefer in an apartment? (a) stained hardwood floors (b) plush carpeted floors (c) floors.
2. Are you responsible about sending thank-you notes?
3. Do you own a pepper grinder?
4. Do you have candles on hand in case of a power failure?
5. Have you recently gotten home from a party at approximately the same time you formerly went out to a party?

—You feel your kitchen is too small.

—You sweat profusely upon being asked, "So, what's new?"

—You read your horoscope.

—You're certain you know more than your boss.

—You can't think of anyone you want to go out drinking with.

—You have lunch with your friend the reporter and decide she has a better job than you.

—You have lunch with your friend the upholstery salesman and decide he has a better job than you.

—You have lunch with your friends who moved to Vermont to "sketch" and decide they have a better life than you.

—You think you would like to open your own restaurant.

—You think you would like to teach English in Japan.

—You think you would like to "get a grant."

—You have already sent away for the Outward Bound catalog.

—The first thing you read in the Sunday paper is the travel section.

—You do not remember the last time you ingested an illegal substance.

—You are considering acupuncture.

—You can't think of anything new to eat for dinner.

—You secretly suspect that you have Epstein-Barr syndrome.

—You have started exercising regularly.

—You have stopped exercising entirely.

—You have been listening to all your old albums.

—You spend an entire evening complaining about your city.

—You spend an entire day in the suburbs and think it is actually kind of nice.

—You wonder what you would look like with shorter hair.

—You wonder what you would look like with longer hair.

—You are thinking of writing a humorous book about life after college.

MID-MIDLIFE CRISIS MANAGEMENT

Never ignore the warning signs of the Mid-Midlife Crisis. If you do, you will experience a *real* midlife crisis twenty-five years from today. And just imagine what people will say *then* when they see you driving recklessly to Mexico in a red Corvette convertible with a hitchhiker half your age. They will say you take after your father.

To avoid this ugly fate, take action now. What you need in your life is change. Sometimes, all it takes is small change, such as quarters. Once you have used this change to do the several months of laundry you're now using as deep-pile bedroom carpet, you will feel[2] much better. Other times, a bigger change is in order, such as a change of scenery. How about hitchhiking to Mexico?

How you have your personal crisis is entirely up to you. But most Mid-Midlifers opt for one of the simple strategies below:

GET MARRIED. Planning a wedding gives you something to take your mind off all your problems: a new set of problems. First you have to find a place to get married. Then you

2 *and smell*

have to find a caterer. And a band. Then you have to decide who to invite. Once you think you've done it all, you have to go out and find someone to marry. Why not call off the wedding and just . . .

GET A DOG. Mid-Midlifers who aren't ready for a spouse often get a pet to help them through their crisis. If the idea appeals to you, adopt one through an animal shelter. This allows you to feel more humanitarian without the hassle of doing volunteer work. If you start feeling guilty about being at work all day while your St. Bernard is trapped in an apartment smaller than his cage at the ASPCA, you need only to . . .

QUIT YOUR JOB. After about four years in the Real working World, you'll finally attain some responsibility and respect. What better time to throw it all away to go flip burgers in Vail? Once you find there are no job openings in Vail, pack your bags and . . .

MOVE TO SEATTLE. Seattle has become a magnet for Lifers in the throes of Mid-Midlife. That is why many people say it is a very homogeneous place. If you prefer conducting your crisis to the beat of a different drummer, flee the grunge horde and . . .

JOIN THE PEACE CORPS. This option is perfect for those seeking an all-out departure from Entry-Level life. Instead of living in a roach-infested apartment, subsisting on a diet of stir-fry chicken, and working for people you resent in the Real World, you get to live in a leech-infested mud hut, subsist on a diet of stir-fry squirrel, and work for people who resent *you* in the *Third* World. Once you've used up all your sick days on that nagging case of malaria, come back home and . . .

TAKE A POTTERY CLASS. Many Mid-Midlifers find that doing something creative is all they really need to resolve their crisis. If you do not like pottery, perhaps you should take up collage, or learn to play the flute. Or perhaps you should pull the trigger of the pistol you have pointed at your head. But first, be sure to do what *all* Mid-Midlifers do when they have tried everything else and still feel that familiar four-year itch . . .

GO BACK TO SCHOOL.

ENTRY-LEVEL ACHIEVEMENT TEST (ELAT)

Directions: The final exam below is designed to test your mastery of the Entry-Level Lifestyle. Fill in each circle completely, using a sharp #2 pencil only. Do not make any stray marks on the exam paper. You will have 15 minutes to finish. When time is called, put your pencil down and close your booklet. No wandering eyes.

1. milk crate:dining room chair as **(a)** Hervé Villechaize:Weezie from *The Jeffersons* **(b)** office baby shower:fun **(c)** rejection letter:kindling   ⓐ   ⓑ   ⓒ

2. "touch base":hook up as **(a)** "telephone tag":duck duck goose **(b)** "FYI":LSD **(c)** "regroup":chill   ⓐ   ⓑ   ⓒ

3. Which is the Real-World memo?   ⓐ   ⓑ   ⓒ
(a) Boner—Out of Brew, Went to Get More.—Stinky
(b) To: B
    Fr: S
    Re: Intoxicant Inventory Control
    B: It has been brought 2 my att., de facto, that the following irregularity has transpired: *supply* < *demand* re: brewed malt & hops beverage allotmnt. Ipso facto, I m presently n-gaged in ad interum rectification of status quo.
    Vis-a-Vis,
    Stnky

4. The most important date to postpone in the Real World is **(a)** a blind date **(b)** your wedding date **(c)** April 15   ⓐ   ⓑ   ⓒ

5. You receive notification that your gas is about to be cut off if you don't pay your heat bill. You: ⓐ   ⓑ   ⓒ
(a) try to use a portable heater but fail because your electricity has been cut off **(b)** try to call the gas company but fail because your phone has been cut off **(c)** move in with your parents

6. You are most comfortable at a party in which you are: **(a)** wearing a vomit-stained toga **(b)** hallucinating **(c)** invited   ⓐ   ⓑ   ⓒ

7. In your pre-Real-World years, you spent a summer as a counselor-in-training at Happy Seashore Day Camp. This experience appears on your résumé as: **(a)** counselor-in-training, Happy Seashore Day Camp **(b)** Imperial Commanding Councilperson and Joint Ambassador Chief of Council, Jocund Coastal Diurnal Encampment   ⓐ   ⓑ   ⓒ

8. Which of the following geometrical forms can be applied to the Real working World formula "X-to-Y," when X = 5 and Y = 9? (a) (b) (c)

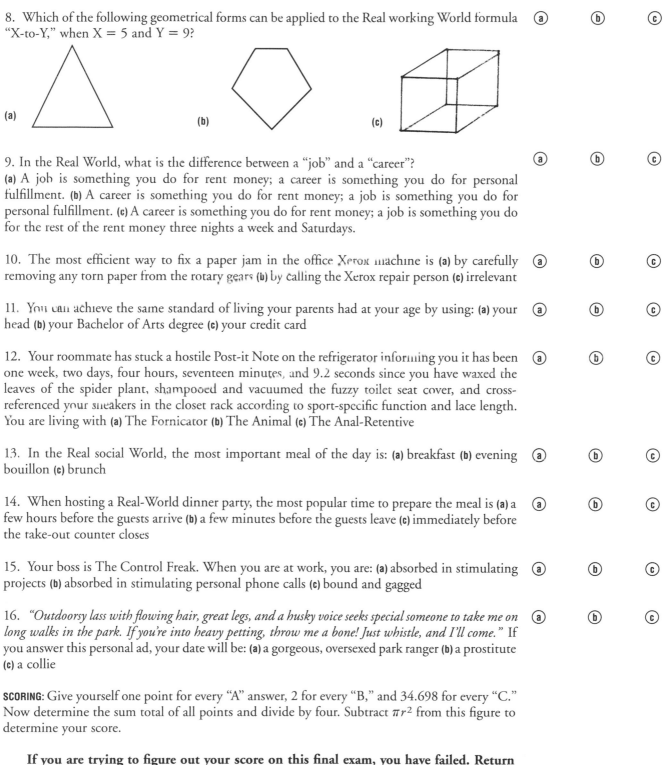

(a)   (b)   (c)

9. In the Real World, what is the difference between a "job" and a "career"? (a) (b) (c)
(a) A job is something you do for rent money; a career is something you do for personal fulfillment. **(b)** A career is something you do for rent money; a job is something you do for personal fulfillment. **(c)** A career is something you do for rent money; a job is something you do for the rest of the rent money three nights a week and Saturdays.

10. The most efficient way to fix a paper jam in the office Xerox machine is **(a)** by carefully removing any torn paper from the rotary gears **(b)** by calling the Xerox repair person **(c)** irrelevant (a) (b) (c)

11. You can achieve the same standard of living your parents had at your age by using: **(a)** your head **(b)** your Bachelor of Arts degree **(c)** your credit card (a) (b) (c)

12. Your roommate has stuck a hostile Post-it Note on the refrigerator informing you it has been one week, two days, four hours, seventeen minutes, and 9.2 seconds since you have waxed the leaves of the spider plant, shampooed and vacuumed the fuzzy toilet seat cover, and cross-referenced your sneakers in the closet rack according to sport-specific function and lace length. You are living with **(a)** The Fornicator **(b)** The Animal **(c)** The Anal-Retentive (a) (b) (c)

13. In the Real social World, the most important meal of the day is: **(a)** breakfast **(b)** evening bouillon **(c)** brunch (a) (b) (c)

14. When hosting a Real-World dinner party, the most popular time to prepare the meal is **(a)** a few hours before the guests arrive **(b)** a few minutes before the guests leave **(c)** immediately before the take-out counter closes (a) (b) (c)

15. Your boss is The Control Freak. When you are at work, you are: **(a)** absorbed in stimulating projects **(b)** absorbed in stimulating personal phone calls **(c)** bound and gagged (a) (b) (c)

16. *"Outdoorsy lass with flowing hair, great legs, and a husky voice seeks special someone to take me on long walks in the park. If you're into heavy petting, throw me a bone! Just whistle, and I'll come."* If you answer this personal ad, your date will be: **(a)** a gorgeous, oversexed park ranger **(b)** a prostitute **(c)** a collie (a) (b) (c)

SCORING: Give yourself one point for every "A" answer, 2 for every "B," and 34.698 for every "C." Now determine the sum total of all points and divide by four. Subtract πr^2 from this figure to determine your score.

If you are trying to figure out your score on this final exam, you have failed. Return immediately to page one. If not, congratulations! You have learned the most important and celebrated lesson of Entry-Level Life: *In the Real World, there are no final exams.*